BRAIN
GAMES
FOR
CATS

CLAIRE ARROWSMITH

FIREFLY BOOKS

A Firefly Book

Published by Firefly Books Ltd. 2016

First printing

Publisher Cataloging-in-Publication Data (U.S.)

Names: Arrowsmith, Claire, author.
Title: Brain games for cats : learn how to stimulate your cat by using the power of play / Claire Arrowsmith.
Description: Richmond Hill, Ontario, Canada : Firefly Books, 2016. I Includes bibiography. I Summary: "This innovative new title aims to show owners of cats how a routine of simple but enriching brain games can make your pet a happier, healthier and more loving companion for life. Brain Games for Cats is a brilliantly conceived compendium of fun games, tricks and activities that you can enjoy with your cat or kitten that will keep him fit and stimulated from an early age" -- Provided by publisher.
Identifiers: ISBN 978-1-77085-764-3 (paperback)
Subjects: LCSH: Cats – Exercise. I Games for cats.
Classification: LCC SF446.7A776 I DDC 636.8083 – dc23

Library and Archives Canada Cataloguing in Publication

Arrowsmith, Claire, author
    Brain games for cats : learn how to stimulate your cat by using the power of play / Claire Arrowsmith.
Includes bibliographical references.
ISBN 978-1-77085-764-3 (paperback)
    1. Games for cats. 2. Cats--Training. I. Title.
SF446.7.A77 2016   636.7'0887   C2016-900043-5

Published in the United States by
Firefly Books (U.S.) Inc.
P.O. Box 1338, Ellicott Station
Buffalo, New York 14205

Published in Canada by
Firefly Books Ltd.
50 Staples Avenue, Unit 1
Richmond Hill, Ontario L4B 0A7

Printed in China

Conceived, designed and produced by

Interpet Publishing, Vincent Lane, Dorking, Surrey RH4 3YX, England

Editor Philip de Ste. Croix; Designer Philip Clucas MCDS; Photographer Roddy Paine; Cat trainer Sue Ottmann; Production management Consortium, Suffolk; Print production 1010 Printing International Ltd

Chapter **ONE**

Understanding Your Cat

CONTENTS

PART 1: PREPARE TO PLAY BRAIN GAMES 6

Chapter **TWO**

Planning to Play Brain Games

Chapter **THREE**

What You Need to Begin Brain Games

CONTENTS continued overleaf ▶

PART 2: BRING ON THE BRAIN GAMES 40

Note on the Text

Brain Games are meant to be played by all cats, both male and female. For ease of readability without gender bias, we have opted to alternate between "he" and "she" pronouns throughout the text.

PREPARE BRAIN

PART ONE

TO PLAY GAMES

UNDERSTANDING YOUR CAT

It is very likely that, as a reader of this book, you have already welcomed cats into your life in some way or another. In fact, cats have become the most popular companion pet in recent years. Their size, adaptability and apparent suitability to our modern way of living has led to more and more homes taking in a cat. There are now believed to be around 600 million domestic cats worldwide.

However, the high number of pet cats given up to rescue, rehomed or presented for behavioral therapy suggests that for many cats something in their current world is falling short of fulfilling what they need to maintain their happiness, health and feline satisfaction.

The aim of this book is not necessarily to create a performing cat, but to help you to spend more time with your cat, to learn more about his or her capabilities and to find ways to provide stimulation and entertainment of the sort your cat enjoys.

FELINE HISTORY

The cat's path from wild ancestor to our household companion is complex and fascinating. The domestic cat is "domesticated" in very loose terms and is unique compared to the other species that we have embraced into our lifestyles as pets or companions.

While the historical data is constantly changing as a result of new discoveries, the current thinking is that cats probably started to be domesticated successfully about 10,000 years ago. This coincided with changes in human habits, since it was at this time that we started to develop agricultural practices and then to store our crops. This habit unsurprisingly started to attract small rodents, now identified as our common house mouse, and these in turn attracted the wild cats of the region. Attempts at domestication appear to have sprung up across the globe, but only the Arabian Wildcat actually went on to become the ancestor for all the cats that we know and love today.

For a long period of time the cat was encouraged around our settlements purely for its hunting skills. We did not control breeding and so as a species they remained relatively unchanged. Some types of cats have altered more than others; for

LEFT Millions of cats are kept as pets around the world. It is fascinating to think that all these house-loving companions descend from a wild ancestor

Humans first appreciated the company of cats because of their hunting abilities

example, the Siamese developed from a small population of domesticated cats that were transported to Southeast Asia before being isolated from further genetic input. This small breeding pool resulted in these cats looking quite distinct from other breeds of domestic cats that we recognize today. However, they still share the same ancestor as our other familiar breed types.

The cat has lived in the U.K. for over 2,000 years. It made its way to the Americas about 500 years ago and finally to Australia 400 years ago. The purpose for domestication remained much the same though; it helped us to control vermin and the cat was small enough to fit easily into our homes, bred quickly, was self-sustaining and required very little human input.

In much more recent times the popularity of restricting breeding pools and breeding

LEFT The distinctive appearance of the Siamese derives from a population that was isolated in the Far East for centuries

cats selectively has gained momentum and approximately 60 breeds are recognized today with several other hybrids, crossbreeds and "type" cats being popular in different areas. While some of these breeds are distinctive looking, genetically there are very few differences and in general cats are similar shapes and sizes.

While the historical background of cats is an interesting subject in itself, you may wonder why it is relevant to a book about cat games.

RIGHT The civilizations of Ancient Egypt revered cats and even worshipped them as deities. Anyone who unwisely killed a cat risked death by execution

The answer is that an understanding of how the familiar domestic cat developed has significant benefits with regard to the way we view them, the way we interact with them and our overall expectations of them. Knowing that we have actually altered cats very little in comparison to their wild ancestors will help to explain why your cat behaves in the way she does. Having a better understanding will then open your mind to exploring ways to satisfy your cat's natural instincts rather than trying to suppress or totally prevent natural feline behavior.

FELINE SENSES

Touch Considering how agile and sensitive your cat is, it will come as no surprise to learn that his tactile senses develop even before birth. Over time your cat has become one of the most agile and sensory-aware animals that we live with. This characteristic can be adapted and utilized in the more physical brain games. While not all cats are keen athletes, it benefits them all to be active and to move around.

Kittens are blind at birth but can sense their mother's smell

ABOVE Cats have a very sensitive sense of smell. A cat uses scent to sniff out food, mates and the presence of rivals and to seek out his own territory, which he has previously marked.

> ▨▨▨ **SAFE SCENTS** ▨▨▨
>
> Some more apprehensive cats can benefit from being exposed to smells that help them to feel safe. Pheromones are naturally occurring substances that an animal excretes that convey an airborne signal to other members of the same species. Synthetic feline pheromones can be purchased and positioned in your home environment via plug-in diffuser sprays. These can help a cat to feel secure and may help him to relax sufficiently to engage in some of the games. Once he is playing and feeling the pleasure engendered by these activities, he should start to naturally feel happier as a result.

Smell Your cat's olfactory ability, or in other words his capability to smell, is highly acute. He is able to detect scent as soon as he is born and by three weeks of age his nose is at full working capacity. His sense of smell is at least 10 times as acute as that of a human and his emotions are highly influenced by the scents he detects. Smell also appears to have a role to play in making food seem attractive, as older cats with a reduced sense of smell can go off their food. Your cat will be able to detect the scent of treats you hide, but since cats are "sit and wait" predators they are often happy to crouch and wait, in hope that this little morsel will appear of its own accord, just as a mouse would. You may have to spend time helping your cat to learn some of the games that require more active participation on the part of the cat.

Paws and whiskers are part of the sense of touch

Hearing When your cat was born he did not possess the acute hearing that he does now. However, by the time he had become more independent at a month of age, he had excellent hearing ability. A cat's hearing is especially adapted to detect the sounds of prey that we are incapable of detecting.

Your cat can hear you very well and so you should avoid shouting or using deep, gruff tones where possible. Cats appear to respond well to higher, more excited tones of voice, "kissy" noises and clucks, but all cats are individual and need to become accustomed to their own humans.

BELOW Cats have a reflective layer behind the retina that bounces light back into the eye. This helps their night vision and causes the wonderful effect of brightly shining eyes

Sight At birth a kitten's eyes are still closed and they only open after approximately one week to 10 days. Again, sight develops very quickly, so that by the time a young cat is moving around more at three weeks he can use sight to provide him with very important information. While he has many senses to help him be the lithe hunter he is, he is excellent at detecting movement.

Lots of brain games for cats will involve fast-moving toys to either lure your cat to follow them or as a reward for correct actions. He might also like to chase rolling toys or flicked treats; be prepared to work with what your cat loves most.

WHY DO CATS "PLAY"?

Play may seem a frivolous use of time, but it has many qualities that enhance an animal in different ways. We know that play allows the cat to develop physically, engaging in activity that increases her strength and overall level of health. In the wild, cats would hunt up to 20 times a day. Although they can also be found

Playing games with a kitten helps with bonding

snoozing for long periods, this routine ensures that the cat remains both physically and mentally active. But a pet's lifestyle means that it can be hard for a cat to find and maintain healthy levels of activity or entertainment without engaging in behaviors that we owners really dislike. Overall we have to remember that play is quite simply fun to do!

Kitten play From approximately four weeks of age a kitten is consumed by the urge to play. This focus will vary between individuals but it will last for several months at least. During this time the kitten develops her physical ability and social skills while she plays with siblings or other family members. A lack of opportunity to play can lead to an adult cat with poor social skills.

Bonding Taking the time to handle and play games with your kitten can help her to mature into a sociable adult cat who will happily interact with you. The time that you spend with her is valuable: it will help you to recognize her abilities and patterns of behavior, and makes it easier for you to detect when she is unwell or injured.

Concerns Many people misunderstand the role that play has in relation to the predatory behavior of their cat. They assume that if they teach their kitten or cat to play, then she will engage in more unwanted predatory activity. Research has shown that this is not the case. While weaning age can influence a cat's hunting performance, whether or not a kitten is played with is not a prediction of future behavior. A kitten does learn which targets she prefers during this time, but since the predatory instinct will develop with or without play anyway, it is the environment that plays the most influential role in what prey the cat encounters and so learns to hunt.

LEFT Play allows a cat to hone the skills that are needed to be a hunter

VITAL EARLY EXPERIENCES

While owners of new puppies are often closely advised about the critical importance of socialization, most kittens unfortunately do not come with such useful guidance. This is a missed opportunity because the early weeks of a kitten's life are very important in relation to the development of future behavior. Up to approximately nine weeks of age a kitten finds it easy to take in new information and to accept new experiences without feeling worried. These early lessons then allow the growing cat to cope with more events without feeling stressed. When kittens are handled for short periods daily, they mature into cats that are more willing to have contact with their owners, to engage in interactive activity and to accept changes to their environments. A few small changes to the pattern of a cat's early experiences can have lifelong impacts.

Starting with an older cat If your cat was not handled much during his early months of life, you may find that he struggles to allow much contact with you. He may startle easily or dislike events that are not predictable. This may well impact on his ability to play with you, but hopefully you will be able to find something to engage his attention. Even if you have to focus on non-contact games, he should be able to discover something that sparks his interest.

RIGHT You can almost hear the purring! A calm, contented cat is a wonderful companion to have around the home.

Perhaps you have owned your cat from an early age and have a nice relationship with him but only infrequently engage in play sessions. While some cats will embrace the fun of new games, it is better to start slowly with such cats to build up interest and enthusiasm, rather than having high expectations of a cat that has not been used to his brain (and body) being stimulated in this way before.

ABOVE If a cat is properly socialized while still a young kitten, he should grow up into a well-balanced adult who is comfortable with the physical contact that owners so enjoy.

HOW DOES YOUR CAT LEARN?

It is often wrongly thought that cats can't be taught to do much. This assumption has come about because cats don't willingly work endlessly for humans. Why should they? As you know, cats were encouraged to live with us to hunt our vermin and we never spent much time selectively breeding them to be really good at any other particular job. Therefore, we have never created a cat with a focus and desire to work like a Border Collie.

ABOVE It takes patience and sensitivity to train a cat, but the rewards of success make it all seem worthwhile

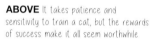

LEFT Cats are innately solitary hunters, we have to teach them how to play games

A cat is, and always has been, a solitary hunter with the ability to make social choices depending on the circumstances she finds herself in. But it is wrong to think that because it is harder to motivate a cat, they are unable to learn at all.

Learning processes You do not need to be an expert in learning theory in order to train your cat to play Brain Games. However, having an understanding of the way your cat processes information will give you an appreciation of why you should work systematically and proceed in particular ways with her. There are many frustrated trainers out there not achieving the desired results because of their bad timing, unrealistic expectations or confusing methods.

Habituation This is an unusual type of learning because it actually involves the loss of a response rather than the acquisition of a new one, which is normally what learning involves. It is important for most animals to learn which things going on around it can be safely ignored, and which should be paid attention to. Habituation occurs when certain events prove to be inconsequential to the individual and so they learn to ignore them — energy and time can be saved for more important things. A cat that has been used to a home environment will be able to relax more easily than one that has not been used to a house, or one that has spent long periods in a cattery, because it knows which noises, smells and objects can be safely ignored. It might take a new cat some time to adjust properly to your domestic routine, so it is better not to try to start Brain Games until your new cat is settled and comfortable in your home.

Sensitization Experiences that cause your cat to feel suddenly scared or startled can lead to an increasing reaction to similar events occurring in the future. It is important for a cat to learn to avoid, or ready herself for, something scary or dangerous, but sometimes this growing sensitivity can lead to problems, as the cat can become over-reactive or worried by things that are not dangerous or threatening in any way.

Classical conditioning This is a very well-known type of learning that is typically linked to the work of the famous Russian scientist Ivan Pavlov, who studied the mechanism of salivation in dogs. We know that this type of learning can be applied to most species including honeybees, pigeons and, of course, our cats. Classical conditioning occurs when a neutral event (something that normally means nothing to your cat) is paired up with another event that naturally causes a reflexive response (which is a response that cannot be controlled, such as salivating when food is presented). Probably the most commonly used pairing is between food and an event. When a neutral event (a noise for example) is repeatedly paired with the food, then eventually the noise by itself will cause the animal to salivate as if the food were present. Once this occurs we consider the conditioning to have been successful.

Operant conditioning When we think of training our cats, this is generally the type of learning that we are talking about. This method is all about the animal learning that it can control the environment by acting in a certain way. So, by performing a certain action the cat can cause a reward to arrive. They learn that actions have consequences, and if the result is a pleasant one (i.e., a reward arrives) then the cat will choose to repeat that action again in the future. Repetition will strengthen the relationship between the action and its result, which is why practicing your Brain Games and making sure that your cat is successful and rewarded for being so will make it easier to succeed in future.

The hand touch or High Five will mean a treat is on the way

ABOVE Technically speaking, we use operant conditioning to teach a cat to play a game. She comes to learn that she can gain a pleasurable reward just by repeating a certain action

PLANNING TO PLAY BRAIN GAMES

WHEN CAN A KITTEN BEGIN TO PLAY?

When awake, a young kitten has little else on his mind other than playing. This play desire remains very high for the first four months before settling down to a degree. After that, there will then be a natural difference in how much each individual cat wants to play, although most continue to play at some level throughout their lives. The time that your cat is prepared to focus on a game will depend on his age and relative experience of playing and training with you. You should start to encourage your kitten to engage with

ABOVE Try to harness a kitten's natural desire to play so that he gets used to the idea of enjoying games with you

you from an early age, in order to build some training patterns into his day and to instill the confidence necessary to try new things. It is unlikely that you will be able to teach him the more complex maneuvers immediately, but by getting started early you have a great opportunity to introduce games into his everyday lifestyle.

WHAT GAMES CAN KITTENS AND CATS PLAY?

Traditionally we think of a cat playing with a small felt mouse, or some wool. Often cats would only be offered these options, particularly when they matured a little. However, the habits of the pet-owning

When the ball starts to move, the game will really begin

ABOVE A game with a moving toy often turns into a wild chase complete with hunting-type pounces and mock "kills."

public have changed over recent years and the vast variety of toys on the market shows that owners do have an interest in buying all sorts of playthings and equipment for their pets' enjoyment. In reality, however, most cat toys are simply placed on the floor for the cat to play with by herself, and there is little more than a brief engagement between owner and cat every now and then. Some of this is understandable; many cats appear to snub new toys or lose interest in play after a few minutes, so owners believe that their cat does not like playing.

TYPES OF PLAY

There are no guarantees about what your cat is going to like doing. Older cats with no history of playing or "problem solving" may never develop a desire to change their habits. However, learning continues throughout an individual's lifetime and so change is always possible. No, your sedentary, nonplayful older cat may never turn into a cat-agility champion but he may love interactive games, embrace the "target" games (see Chapter 8), or simply enjoy performing some of the easier toy-orientated games given some time and patience. Without trying to enjoy

some games together, you will never know what your cat's potential can be.

Cats engage in different types of play, some dependent on the stage of life they have reached and the types of opportunity available to them.

Fast-moving lures will get kittens scampering about in no time

ABOVE Kittens who are littermates will generally play together naturally. It is part of the way they learn about the world

Social play Play with siblings or the mother is the first type to become established. It helps to teach the kitten about his physical abilities and to enhance social bonding. Play between cats will continue if siblings live together, or if a kitten is introduced to another young cat. However, genuine play between unrelated adult cats is a much less common event.

LEFT An activity game, like chasing a lure, allows a cat to run, stretch, leap and swipe with her paws in the safety of her own home.

ABOVE Cats can become totally fascinated by object-centered games, particularly if the plaything moves around in front of them.

Solitary play When littermates are not available, or group play has been exhausted for the time being, a kitten will engage in play activities by himself. This is still beneficial, as he continues to expend energy and develop his physical skills.

GAMES CATS WILL PLAY

Object games These involve any prop, toy or object that your cat may interact with. Cats can develop their fine motor skills by playing with smaller objects, and can entertain themselves with toys either made or purchased for them. These games will fulfill many feline needs and will occupy younger cats for a considerable length of time if the play object, or range of objects, suits the individual.

Activity games Some play involves being active with running, jumping, stretching and pouncing. Younger cats will often indulge in this type of game and it appears to help them to use up energy and to develop fitness at the same time.

Mental games Games that involve more cognitive involvement need more thought by you to set up. Your cat will need to learn what action, or series of actions, results in the arrival of rewards and so your timing will need to be appropriate. Repetition will be required for your cat to learn how to play these games successfully.

ARE BRAIN GAMES SAFE?

Puppy owners are often concerned about avoiding any strenuous activity that could harm the growing joints of their pet. While kittens can be very delicate and care should always be taken, they are naturally more physically capable of activity at an earlier age than a dog. Kittens have to learn to hunt by themselves early on, since after weaning is completed they have to start actively pursuing their own food sources. Kittens are therefore naturally active and energetic during their early months. While it is never a good idea to encourage your kitten to leap from great heights or to play any physically rough games, it should be safe for them to take part in most sensible play and any introductions to Brain Games. You will always be encouraged in this book to choose a safe area to play, free from dangers and distractions. While there are strong benefits to working on a raised platform or surface, you must remain on

LEFT While this book is not suggesting that you try to teach your cat math, certain games do require a degree of mental interaction that helps the cat to develop her cognitive skills

BELOW A raised surface allows you to work with your cat at a comfortable height But be careful if the game speeds up — you don't want any tumbles

the ball and observant to prevent your kitten from taking any unexpected tumbles off the edges of the tabletop.

If you have any concerns about your cat or kitten's health and well-being, please discuss these with your veterinarian as soon as possible.

CAUSES FOR LACK OF INTEREST

Fear A cat that has not been socialized thoroughly with people will find it more of a struggle to interact and accept close contact later on. A new kitten or cat may take some time and gentle encouragement in order to relax and feel safe enough to play.

Wrong type of play Your cat may have specific likes and dislikes. Explore different options several times on different days to see what he likes. Watching him closely will give you some idea of the things that catch his attention and get him most excited.

Low energy Playing uses a lot of energy and kittens and active cats can easily tire if they are not getting the right nutrition to support their physical activities.

Social pressure Some cats will be inhibited from playing if another cat is present. This may be due to underlying social problems, prior experience of altercation or competition over interaction with you, or play objects and so on. Consider this when choosing where to play with your cat.

Illness If your cat's willingness to play with you suddenly drops off, or you notice personality or physical changes, do not ignore them. There are many reasons why your cat may be less motivated by food or unable to move around as usual and this must be explored as soon as you notice it.

IS PLAY ONLY FOR KITTENS?

Certainly kittens and young cats are more likely to be keen to play and will probably learn the Brain Games more readily than older individuals. Cats of all ages can be encouraged to play, but you should consider each cat as a unique personality and think about her particular life experiences when you embark on any new routine. Older cats have a naturally lower desire to engage in play activity. This is a biologically appropriate change for a cat and this inclination should be recognized. There are various underlying reasons for this change in play desire, including age-related physical changes that may mean that movement is not as comfortable as it once was. If your cat has slowed down, is not jumping up onto furniture like she once was, or is much slower on the stairs,

then please discuss this with your vet, as there may be treatment options available to make her feel more comfortable once again.

Play allows a kitten to learn in a safe way about events in the environment. Leaping around causes contact with new things, triggering movement and sounds that were not expected. All this teaches a kitten to cope with real-life events that are not always predictable.

INDIVIDUAL PREFERENCES

Your cat's personality This will influence the type of Brain Games that he finds exciting. Personality, or temperament, is influenced by a number of factors that include your cat's genetics, the health and well-being of the mother during pregnancy and after giving birth, and the early life experiences of the kitten. His health and later learning opportunities will impact on how he responds as an adult cat.

Genetics Parental temperament and other traits are clearly very important when we consider how the offspring are likely to behave. We know that young kittens find it easier to learn when their mother is present, and so her tendency to be friendly and relaxed around both people and a variety of situations will positively influence them. Since fathers rarely have any contact with the kittens they produce, it is often

ABOVE Kittens naturally play games at high intensity and use up vast amounts of energy quite quickly. Don't be surprised if they suddenly tire and decide to stop playing

ABOVE If the mother is calm and friendly around people, it is more likely that the kitten will also be easily socialized.

not considered to be particularly relevant to know about his personality. However, research has shown that the father's tendency to be friendly toward people, or "bold," is strongly correlated with the kittens' friendliness.

Socialization Between approximately two and seven weeks of age, a kitten is particularly receptive to learning about social interaction with humans. Therefore, it is very important that during these early weeks the breeder is gently handling the kittens on a daily basis. This teaches the kittens to include humans in their social template. If a kitten does not have contact with people during this early, sensitive period of development, he is highly unlikely ever to be able to interact fully and in the relaxed manner that most owners desire from their cat. In order for your cat to relax enough to play a range of Brain Games, to feel confident to approach you and to allow contact with you, he will require

reasonable social skills and the ability to cope with some novelty.

THE BENEFITS OF SOCIALIZATION

Socialization helps to increase the tolerance and coping mechanisms that cats have to accommodate the "human" desire to make physical contact, lift them up and cuddle them as pets. Naturally, as cats are a vulnerable prey species, these are all types of interaction that they would instinctively find stressful.

Cats learn to accept close contact with humans — it is not innate

Breed tendencies While our domestic cats have nowhere near the variability that we have bred into the domestic dog, it is a fact that there are differences between breeds of cats and this may influence the types of games your cat enjoys most. But don't typecast any cat just by looking at its breed type alone. Within every breed there exists a whole spectrum of personalities and abilities. However, when considering the likelihood of a cat enjoying a particular activity, some breeds are more likely to be successful than others.

ABOVE The natural athleticism and grace of the Bengal makes him suited to fast-moving games with lots of interaction

Persians are renowned for their serene temperaments

ABOVE Persians don't have the get-up-and-go personalities of Bengals — you should find more laid-back games to keep them amused

The high-energy, socially demanding and athletic Bengals are very likely to be successful in the majority of the suggested Brain Games in this book. For many owners, directing their Bengal's energy and enthusiasm for life into a range of appropriate games is a necessary strategy to manage their cat. At the other end of the scale are the more laid-back Persians. While not discounting active games entirely (for they are still cats), you may find that this breed that loves social contact will adore the activities that require less climbing and more targeted focus.

Breeds such as the Bengal and Turkish Van are often known to seek out water for fun. They might like to rush to the sink when a tap is turned on, play in water bowls or dip paws, sometimes disastrously, into vases. However, it is important that they are not forced to have contact with water and that any water games are carefully introduced. But cats from these types of breeds are less likely to rebel at the concept than many others.

Of course, most pet cats fall into the generic "house cat" category which indicates a heritage involving no obvious single main breed. For this reason, the majority of us cannot rely on breed type when considering what Brain Games such a cat may like most. We have to concentrate (as all owners should, no matter what breed is involved) on raising our cats correctly, spending time with them to build mutual trust and to learn about their likes and dislikes, and having patience in our attempts to find different ways to play with them successfully.

BRAIN GAMES SHOULD BE FUN

Overall, no matter how successful you are as a trainer, or how able your cat is to learn, you should aim to have fun while playing together. The fact that you are trying to engage and learn about your pet is a bonus and will help to strengthen the human-animal bond that you have together.

Where should you play? Remember that the best performance will come when

your cat is feeling confident and happy. This means that you should choose an area of your home where your cat is relaxed, and where she is free from distractions. Cats can feel vulnerable while on the floor, particularly when we are trying to teach

ABOVE Some cats show an interest in water and, of course, the presence of fish is always tempting. But take care — accidents can happen and the consequences can be serious.

them something new, or when taking part in an activity that requires us to lean over them. For this reason, it is suggested that you try to teach the new games and lessons while your cat is on a raised platform. You can use a table, work surface or counter, chair, bed, windowsill; wherever your environment allows, as long as your cat feels happy there and there is sufficient room for her to move and turn around (see Chapter 3 for more information on what you need to play).

When should you play with your cat?

To choose the best time to play with your cat, you should pay attention to her natural pattern of activity. While feral cats are mainly nocturnal, our domestic cat has altered its activity patterns to better suit life with humans. Cats remain a crepuscular species, which means they are most active around dawn and dusk, but the individual cat's activity is highly influenced by her human owner's routine. To be in the right mood to play, your cat should be feeling well and not distracted by a need to go out, or to use the litter tray. A tired cat is less inclined to engage in play and the window of opportunity for playing games can be quite short since a cat may sleep away 15 or more hours every day!

Does your play style suit your cat?

Social play involves both action and response from more than one individual. During Brain Games your cat is relying on you to be a playmate who is trustworthy and fun to spend time with. This will require patience, awareness of when your cat is tiring or becoming less interested, and a willingness to make the experience rewarding for your cat. Accepting the style of play that suits your cat best and building on those skills will be important.

Are you feeling frustrated? Teaching

your cat a new game or trick will take patience. Cats typically have short attention spans for training

sessions and so you will need to start out with the right expectations. Plan for very short sessions at first and be ready to take breaks in between each session. You must wait for your cat to be in the mood to play. Getting the timing right and gauging the appropriate level of difficulty of the session can take a bit of practice when you first start to play Brain Games. If you realize this from the start, you will save yourself from starting to feel frustrated at any lack of progress. It is important to be realistic too. You may have high aspirations for your game playing, but perhaps your cat is content with much simpler activities. If you remain calm and reward all success, then you will make progress within the realms of your cat's individual abilities.

BELOW What if you are ready to play but the time just isn't right? Don't force the issue, if your cat does not want to play, accept it and try again later

BELOW Playtime is only really going to click for your cat if you are both enjoying what you are doing. Try to avoid becoming too goal driven as you introduce a new game — the point is to have fun with your pet, not to win medals for obedience.

ARE YOU BOTH HAVING FUN?

You should both enjoy the play sessions together and if you don't, then it is time to take a break. You might need to focus on a different challenge, choose a different toy or alter the game in a way that makes it more enjoyable for both of you. Always keep in mind the cardinal rule that Brain Games should be fun.

Ensuring your cat has choice Trying to force your cat to play will result in an almost immediate fail. Cats do not have an inherent social structure that has caused them to evolve to appease one another, or to do something just to keep another individual happy. Therefore, if your cat does not enjoy the game or has had enough for one session, you should accept this and allow him to stop, rather than plowing on fruitlessly. This is an important lesson for you as the "trainer" to learn.

For how long have you been playing? Perhaps future sessions can be a little shorter so that you can end the session on a happy note before your cat shows signs of becoming fed up. It may help to slow down the pace at which you try to introduce more difficult tasks, so that your cat becomes confident at each stage of the game. Conversely, for some very able cats you may want to make the level more challenging more quickly.

Why was your cat not enjoying the session? Consider what outside distractions were perhaps disturbing him, whether he needed a break, what time of day it was and how that fit in with your cat's natural routine, what the game was that you were trying to teach and why your cat may not have felt sufficiently rewarded for his efforts. A bit of honest analysis of whether you were doing a good job as a trainer will help to promote more successful play next time.

WHAT YOU NEED TO BEGIN BRAIN

THE IMPORTANCE OF REWARDS

As was described in Chapter 1, a cat learns by pairing up experiences (classical conditioning) or by recognizing that one deliberate action leads to a particular result (operant conditioning). While training your cat to play Brain Games, the aim is to maximize the likelihood that she will give the desired response in the right place and at the right time. The best way to do this is to ensure that when she does get the response right, or at least makes

an effort to try to respond appropriately, you are ready to offer attractive rewards immediately. To reinforce, or reward, an action will strengthen it and make it much more likely to occur again; this is exactly what we want while training for a Brain Game.

Food rewards are the most common choice while training. They are naturally reinforcing; after all, each of us, including our cats, takes pleasure from eating something succulent!

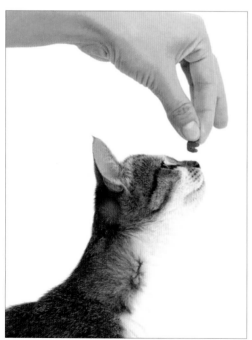

ABOVE Tiny items of food usually make satisfying rewards that let your cat know that she has got an action right

Choice of reward First of all, it is imperative that your cat is being fed a good-quality diet that is suitable for her age and physical requirements. A cat's preferences are established early on in her life, and if a kitten is only presented with a very limited choice of flavor and texture in her foods, then it is likely that she will be a fussier adult eater and less willing

GAMES

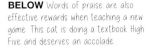

BELOW Words of praise are also effective rewards when teaching a new game. This cat is doing a textbook High Five and deserves an accolade.

to try new things when they are offered to her. This can pose some challenges when training, but the majority of owners can generally find something that their cat enjoys to reward her with, since all cats eat. In this way, the play activity can potentially be sufficiently rewarding for it to be willingly repeated (although this can be a problem if you are trying to train something more challenging that requires multiple repetitions to achieve).

BELOW Experiment with different options to see which treats will best motivate your cat. Tear slices of ham or chicken into small, bite-size fragments.

Options Cat treats come in an array of options. You should choose something that either comes in small pieces, or that can be broken up into small pieces for the training sessions. Cats are designed to consume small prey items, so large treats will fill them up too quickly, take too long to consume and reduce the options for repetition.

It is often helpful to have a variety of options up your sleeve so that your cat does not become bored too quickly with any one reward. Avoid offering your cat chocolate or other human snacks (whether sweetened or salted) as treats. These are potentially harmful to her health.

Praise should be a natural part of training your cat. You may have to alter your normal tone to have the best impact, but using verbal praise will help you to engage with your cat and will strengthen the bond between you.

RIGHT Waving a brightly colored wand toy around is a great way to get a kitten or cat's attention. It often leads to very active chase games, but excitement levels can sometimes boil over. This is not ideal if you need your cat to be calm and collected.

Toys can sometimes be used as a reward for cats that are less motivated to eat treats time after time. While it can be very useful to use a toy for more active games, and a game with a toy can be chosen to reward your cat for performing a somewhat less exciting action first, there are certain challenges with using this type of reward.

- Once your cat has the toy, you will have to accept a break in training while she plays. For the toy to be a real "reward," she should be allowed to play with it in the way she likes most. Giving her the toy and then taking it away again when you want to move on

with the game could actually put her off re-engaging with you.

- A toy may create higher excitement levels that you would prefer to reserve for training or playing a more focused Brain Game. This could interfere with your cat's ability to concentrate on the lesson and may result in unwanted behavior triggered by frustration.

Giving the reward The timing of a reward is very important when considering the impact that it will have on the training results. The more closely an action and reward are paired together, the easier it is for your cat to understand the lesson. If you wait too long, your cat could have performed several other actions that you don't want to encourage (looking around, stepping away, licking her lips) and this could confuse the overall message. You should therefore be ready to offer a reward as soon as your cat gets the game right.

BELOW All these toys can stimulate a cat's natural chase instincts as she uses paws and teeth to trap the "prey."

BELOW When you start training a new game, keep the treat in your hand so that you can reward an action immediately

action, since it will likely be too difficult for your cat to perform the entire response correctly at her first attempt. By rewarding progressively better responses, you will reach your target successfully and with a minimum of stress.

RESPONDING TO MISTAKES

Don't be in any doubt that training a cat can be very frustrating at times. Your cat may not be in the mood, might have only limited focus on your games and sometimes might not be willing to engage with you at all. These are fairly common experiences to have with pet cats that are learning new things.

Be aware of your feelings of frustration and do not let them negatively affect your interactions with your cat. Using an angry voice will not bring your cat around to wanting to play more with you.

To begin with you might need to actually hold the treat in your hand to encourage your cat to respond, and you should also offer verbal praise at the same time. As you and your cat improve with any given game, you can start to encourage her while the treat remains safely in a treat pot or treat pouch, or in your pocket. This will help her to learn to respond without the lure of the food, which could potentially distract from the other cues you are trying to teach. By this stage your cat will be so used to hearing the words of praise from you when she is rewarded that she will feel very pleased with herself when she hears you tell her she is "Good."

Initially you might have to settle for rewarding approximations of the final

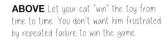

ABOVE Let your cat "win" the toy from time to time. You don't want him frustrated by repeated failure to win the game.

RIGHT If the body language says "I'm too tired," try again later

Punishment This is not the way to improve your relations with your cat, or to increase his desire to work with you. **Punishment will not be successful.** Your cat will very quickly decide that you are not a playmate after all and will engage in more avoidance and solitary behavior. Since cats can naturally survive perfectly well by themselves, they do not place themselves willingly into situations where interactions are likely to be unpleasant.

If your cat finds himself in a situation where he anticipates that punishment might occur, he will reduce play behavior, be more likely to attempt to leave, or possibly even become defensive, which could place you at risk from cat scratches or bites.

Reassess If a mistake has been made, or your cat is doing something other than what you wanted, take a break to give yourself time to think about what is going wrong. You might even want to video yourself training your cat, as this will help you to understand your body language, and perhaps to pick up on signs

> ▬▬ **TIP** ▬▬
> Modern technology such as camera phones allows us to record our training sessions very easily. The results are immediately available for playback so that we can scrutinize and improve our performances straight after the event.

from your cat's body language that you might have missed when concentrating on the training. You may notice something that will help you to understand why the problem is occurring.

ENCOURAGING PLAY BEHAVIOR

Everything you encourage your cat to do must be considered carefully at first. It is vital that all games and props are enjoyable and pose no risk to your cat. No matter how familiar you are with your cat, you should remember that cats, as a species, are highly sensitive

ABOVE The camera on your cell phone is a valuable training tool. You can check your technique at the touch of a button

HOW TO ENCOURAGE PLAY BEHAVIOR

To do	To avoid
Use an encouraging, high-pitched tone of voice to entice your cat to approach. Your cat will have her own preferences; a "pusspuss" sound is commonly used to entice our cats.	Picking up your cat in an attempt to engage with her. Some cats will jump on your shoulder or relax in your arms, but given a choice, many prefer not to be held like this.
Use a wand toy manipulated in fast, jerky movements to motivate your cat to get involved in more active games.	Trying to prolong games when your cat is attempting to leave or is disinterested.
Use rewards and offer them frequently for all successful attempts at a game.	Cuddling or kissing as a reward or to show your pleasure at your cat's performance. These are not actions that a cat finds naturally enjoyable.
Keep play sessions short.	Shouting, smacking or punishing your cat for making mistakes.

to potential threats. This can be attributed to the fact that, despite being excellent hunters themselves, they are naturally preyed upon by many other types of animals including dogs, large birds of prey and other bigger carnivores. Historically, cats have also been the victims of intense persecution by humankind. In many areas, populations have been hunted to extinction, trapped for their pelts or culled simply because they were the focus of superstition and folklore. In addition to these good reasons for the cat to be a wary and sensitive creature, we should recognize the fact that inter-feline relations can

ABOVE Cat fights are notoriously loud and ferocious — we should not be surprised that cats are sometimes wary around us, as they have to cope with a world full of potential risks

involve risky disputes that result in physical violence. All of these factors should make us more fully appreciate the need for thought and consideration in our interactions with cats.

CHOICE OF EQUIPMENT

Brain Games can involve a range of items that you have available in your home. It is vital that all games are safe, so before starting a game, please examine the items you are considering and determine whether they are suitable for the job or not.

BELOW Many cats seem to prefer learning a new game while standing on a raised surface rather than being down on the floor with you

RIGHT A deft flick of a toy on a string often encourages a cat to stretch high to reach it

The surface should be nonslippery and set at a height that is safe for the age and physical health of your cat to work on. Make sure it is stable and consider using a nonslip mat or some bedding to increase your cat's feeling of comfort and security when on it.

Raised platform As was mentioned in Chapter 2, cats perform much more confidently when they are taught up on a raised surface, particularly if you are standing up alongside them while teaching the game. For this reason, you may wish to prepare a table, a counter, a bed or a raised cat play center for the lesson. Wherever you choose, your cat must feel secure. If you normally scold your cat for jumping up on the table or work surface, then this is not an ideal place to start. Your cat may struggle to understand when he is and is not allowed in this place and he may become anxious as a result of your inconsistency.

Working on the floor Some confident cats will work with their owner at floor level. It can help if you are sitting down and are avoiding any actions that will cause you to lean over your cat while you play. This position is also more successful when there are no other cats, children or dogs (even friendly ones) that may interrupt the session and cause distraction.

Toys Cat toys come in multiple shapes and styles to suit all the ways that cats like to play. Always check for damage before you start a play session and dispose of any with parts that could inadvertently be swallowed, or that have become broken and sharp. Cats can accidentally swallow small toys, and items like elastic bands and twist ties. Lengths of wool or string can also cause serious problems when ingested.

HOW TO ENCOURAGE PLAY BEHAVIOR

Small toys perfect for chasing, retrieving or hiding in boxes or cardboard tubes.	Small furry toys, Ping-Pong balls, feather toys, crinkle balls, bell balls, catnip toys.
Toys to encourage climbing, scratching, stretching and jumping.	Cat trees, large scratching posts, logs, hoops.
Interactive toys to encourage action.	Wand toys, target sticks, toys on rope, larger soft toys.
Items to encourage feelings of feline security.	Cardboard boxes, paper bags, cat igloos, raised platforms.

If your cat seems wary of new items, then try to introduce toys well in advance of any attempts to use them for training.

CLICKER TRAINING

While it is not essential for Brain Game training, this technique can help a cat to understand exactly what it is that you want her to do by allowing you to "mark" the specific moment when she gets it right.

A clicker is a simple gadget, usually made from plastic with a metal tongue that emits a "click" sound when it is pressed. This sound means nothing to your cat at first but, through the repeated process of clicking and then offering a treat, the noise becomes paired with the arrival of food. In this way it becomes a signal to your cat that a reward is coming her way. Keeping the message clear for your cat is very important, since if she is in doubt, or rewards are missed, she will quickly lose interest. The benefits of using the clicker include the ability to precisely indicate to your cat when she gets it right, even when you are not standing directly next to her. This is helpful for cats who are performing games that cause them to move away from you (such as some of the targeting games), or for cats that are more comfortable when you are not too close to them. Another positive aspect of clicker training is that it makes you look for the right responses so you can click, rather than focusing on the mistakes.

BELOW The secret to clicker training is to pair the sound of the click (**1**) with the prompt arrival of a food reward (**2**). Once this association is established in the cat's mind, she will realize that a click signals a desirable action

1

2

Initially you should click and reward frequently and for each successful step. As your cat improves, you can expect more from her before the click-reward arrives. While it should be possible to build up so that your cat is performing a whole trick or game before the reward arrives, do not rush to remove the rewards too quickly. Cats need lots of motivation to put the effort into games and so, unless you have a very keen, energetic cat that is bursting with enthusiasm, expect to continue to "pay" your cat for her active participation!

ABOVE Targets can take many forms, such as a place mat, a plastic disk or a ball on the end of a target stick. The clicker is used to "mark" the moment when the target is touched.

learn to touch an item (called the target) with his paw or his nose in order to earn the reward. Your timing as the trainer has to be precise in order to teach this, but — once mastered — there really is unlimited fun to be had with the technique — your imagination is the main limiting factor!

TARGET TRAINING

This is a name for a style of training that involves teaching your cat (or any animal) to perform a particular action in a particular place. For example, the cat may

BELOW Successful target training uses the click-treat technique outlined on page 33. Here a paw touch earns the cat a treat.

What to use as a target? A training target can literally be almost anything. You can use a square of paper, a Post-it note, a coaster, a target stick (a stick with a ball or area at the end that you teach your cat to touch), a wooden post, a mat, even a flyswatter! Cats have even been taught to "target," or touch, a small coin and to move a considerable distance in order to do this. With sufficient practice your cat is likely to be able to learn to target something too.

Depending on what you would like your cat to learn to do, your choice of target may change. For example, if you want your cat to use his paw to touch a coaster, you would not also use this coaster for a training game that required him to sit on it. It is much less confusing for your cat if you change the target when you change the task.

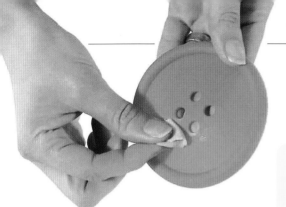

ABOVE If your cat at first does not seem particularly interested in your chosen target, it helps to rub some of his favorite food on it to make it more tempting to explore.

TIP

Do you want to get your cat to do more than touch? If you want him to scratch or scrabble at a target, you could start with a clear plastic mat and place a treat underneath. Be ready to click and treat your cat for starting to scratch at the mat. Build this up so that your cat is scrabbling reliably before removing the treat completely.

Getting started Your cat may be naturally interested in the chosen target and will come forward to investigate. If not, you may need to rub a little food on it to attract his interest, or move it in such a way that he takes notice. You can then use your clicker to begin to shape the behavior you want to encourage.

Fading the target Once your cat is confidently touching the target in the way you would like, you can increase the difficulty by either moving it farther away, or perhaps by making it smaller. Some owners like eventually to have a particular action trained, and then to remove the target entirely. This is possible with cats that have become very competent at responding to your signal to go and touch the target. It would not be sensible to try

to fade out the target until this stage has been achieved and your cat is performing the game very confidently.

One way to remove the need for the target is to position it farther away from the point where you actually want your cat to go to or to touch. As your cat moves toward the target, he will arrive at the place where you want him to end up. Be quick! You will need to be ready to click or praise at that exact moment **before** he passes the chosen spot. Reward him at that stage so that going to this place becomes a rewarding action by itself. With repetition, he will start to expect the reward to come in that specific place, rather than when he touches the actual target.

Remember that you continue to use your click-treat or praise for correct responses, even when the target has been faded out.

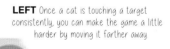

LEFT Once a cat is touching a target consistently, you can make the game a little harder by moving it farther away.

PROBLEMS DURING BRAIN GAMES

Fear Some more anxious cats can display fear of new items brought in to the home. Usually you can overcome this by placing the unfamiliar object somewhere unobtrusive for a few days and allowing your cat to explore in her own time. Given time, most cats will habituate to new items and you can then begin to move the items into new locations and involve them in fun games. If your cat is particularly worried by noise, then choose quieter games, avoid loud, enthusiastic praise and opt for a quieter clicker (there are some tiny ones available that are less likely to startle a sensitive cat).

Spraying on items Urine spray marking is a natural feline behavior in both males and females. It signals important messages to other cats about territory, the presence of another cat and so on. Normally this would only occur around the outer edges of a territory and so not within the home environment, which is considered the core

> **FELINE PHEROMONE THERAPY**
>
> Newly introduced cats, or those adjusting to changes in their environment, may benefit from the use of feline pheromones that can help to safely create a positive emotional response in the cat. They dispense a synthetic version of a cat's natural pheromones into the air and come as a plug-in diffuser for the home, or as sprays which can be applied to items directly.

territory, where a cat should feel at her most secure. Indoor spraying is generally a sign that all is not well with your cat and that they perceive a threat of some sort within the home. If your cat is spraying on the new toys or items you are bringing in to play with, she may be worrying about these novel items. You can remedy this concern by observing your cat carefully when things are first brought home. Try rubbing familiar scents onto the worrisome item via a cloth that has first been used to rub down your cat, or perhaps that your cat has slept on. This may help to hide the "newness" of the item. If the spraying habit is frequent, or occurs throughout your home, then professional help is available — contact your veterinarian for advice.

LEFT Cats normally use their litter trays if they cannot get outside to urinate. Spray marking around the house is different and may indicate that the cat is troubled.

ABOVE Some high-intensity games can get a cat very excited and if you are working close to her, there's a risk that your hands will suddenly become targets for biting

Biting Some owners report that their cat might suddenly bite them during play. Often this occurs when the cat is very excited, and can be a redirection of her energies from the toy to the hand that is closest to her. In such cases it can help if you are careful of your movements, use wand toys or stay out of range during active games. Other cats will bite when they become frustrated. This can happen if the cat is confused and expecting a reward that has not arrived. To avoid this, please work slowly through the various stages of a game, making sure that your cat is successful at each stage before moving on to the next. Never push her to improve too quickly and don't change the goal

markers within a session unless your cat is very used to learning new things and you are confident that she is relaxed and comfortable with what is going on.

Using claws When excited, some cats will use their claws during play. This is more likely if they are playing a predatory game, but some cats are typically less "careful" than others. Remain aware of your cat's behavior, keep hands and feet away from her when she is overexcited and try to calm the game down before this happens. Never continue a game if your cat is grabbing at your body or clothing with her claws. If she learns that doing this will cause the fun to

LEFT Kittens have very sharp claws that often come into play when they are particularly excited

37

end and you will promptly remove yourself from the scene, then she should be less likely to repeat this response in future.

If your cat is fearful and using her claws defensively (to make you stop or go away), then you should stop playing and review your methods before continuing. You must identify the reasons for the fear and address those as a priority. Brain Games are meant to be fun and it will be counterproductive to keep playing if your cat is becoming distressed.

> **TAKE CARE**
>
> If your cat is behaving in a way that concerns you, causes injury or seems excessively fearful, then please talk to your veterinarian who can help you to find an appropriate feline behavior specialist.

A cat's natural grace and athleticism are very clear to see when she is playing

BELOW A cat's claws have three main functions in the wild. They allow her to grip onto objects when climbing, they are used to grasp prey when hunting, and they are a potent defense weapon when she has to fight off a predator. When they are not in use, they retract into sheaths between the toe pads

Cats and owners will both benefit from spending time playing Brain Games together

BRAIN GAME GUIDELINES

As you work through this book you will notice that for each Brain Game there are some additional suggestions in a colored panel to help you to prepare before you begin. Having everything you need and starting in the right place is important to ensure an undisrupted and successful play session.

The key represents the following:

 = cat plays game with owner

 = cat plays alone

Location This is a suggestion of the type of location to which this game is best suited.

Level of difficulty This is a difficulty ranking based on how hard each game is, using a star system where 1 star = Beginner Level and 3 stars = Advanced. However, remember it is only a guide. Everything depends to a great extent on your cat's personality, ability and mood at the time. Use it as a guide, and if you are just starting out, try some of the 1 star games first.

Interactive level This is a quick-scan visual aid so that you can flick through the games and immediately find some that your cat can enjoy by himself, and others that involve your participation. This may be helpful when you are looking for things to occupy your cat while you are busy with work or family, or when you specifically want something to challenge you both and help you to build a stronger bond.

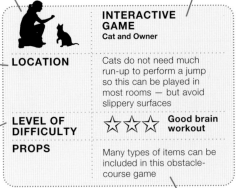

	INTERACTIVE GAME Cat and Owner
LOCATION	Cats do not need much run-up to perform a jump so this can be played in most rooms — but avoid slippery surfaces
LEVEL OF DIFFICULTY	☆☆☆ Good brain workout
PROPS	Many types of items can be included in this obstacle-course game

Props This is a list of the suggested items required for playing the specific game. For some, you may only need a few nice treats, but for others you might have to gather some items in order to create the game properly.

BRING
BRAIN

PART TWO

ON THE
GAMES

GAMES FOR LESS ACTIVE CATS

KITTY SIT

While this is a lesson most pet dogs are taught, cat owners tend not to focus on this type of interaction with their cat. However, you might be surprised to find that it is fairly easy to teach your cat to sit with at least some degree of reliability. Sitting comes so naturally to a cat that you are likely to have lots of opportunity to encourage the action and link it to your cue word.

1 Begin when your cat is showing some interest in interacting with you. She might be asking for attention or for some food — either way she will be more likely to respond to your lesson. If your cat is relaxed on the floor, sit or crouch down so that you are comfortable and not leaning over her. Some cats feel happier learning on a raised surface, so you may wish to start on a table or a windowsill. Hold a treat close to your cat's nose and allow her to sniff it.

	INTERACTIVE GAME Cat and Owner	
LOCATION	Where your cat feels relaxed	
LEVEL OF DIFFICULTY	☆ Easy brain exercise	
PROPS	Some tempting treats	

A cat's body language can tell you quite a lot about how she is feeling. When a cat sits up and is attentive to her surroundings, she is normally calm and relaxed but still switched on to what is going on around her.

4 When your cat is coming and sitting easily, you can begin to add in a verbal command, "Sit," just as her bottom touches the floor each time. Getting your timing right will help your cat to link the verbal command with the action.

 TIP
Stay relaxed and avoid manually pushing your cat's bottom toward the floor. This will only cause her to dislike the interaction, and undermine your chances of success.

2 Taking the movement very slowly and steadily, raise the treat upward and backward over your cat's head so that her nose rises to follow it. Cats are very flexible, but normally, as their heads raise to follow the treat, their bottoms will lower down toward the ground. You may need to practice to find the perfect angle of movement that gets your cat into the correct position.

3 Release the treat as soon as your cat's bottom touches the floor, and offer praise. Linking the reward with the desired position will encourage your cat to opt for this position more quickly the next time.

Practice this routine a few times when your cat comes for her meal or some attention. You should find it becomes easier and faster to get her into the "Sit" position.

5 The "Sit" position can be prolonged by offering another reward while she is still in position. Of course, a cat might remain sitting for a long period simply because she feels like it, and she likes the view, but it is still fun to be able to elicit a response on cue.

6 Tidbits are useful training aids and a cat is quite likely to respond to a specific command for the reward of a tasty treat. Over time you can phase them out, so that a verbal cue or hand signal is all you need.

Practice in different places around your home and with different people present, so that your cat learns to respond even with distractions. Even young kittens can learn this game if you are patient with them.

FLAT CAT!

We are used to our cats sprawling out on the floor in sunbeams or on comfy beds, but adding a simple instruction such as "Down" can appear rather impressive when most cats are not taught any such cue. As well as being one part of an extensive repertoire of activities and lessons to enjoy with your cat, being able to easily get him into a "Down" position can make grooming and general examination easier.

1 Choose a time when your cat is relaxed and willing to interact with you. He should be in a place where he can easily lie down, this might be on the floor or up on a raised surface

	INTERACTIVE GAME Cat and Owner
LOCATION	A place where your cat feels safe
LEVEL OF DIFFICULTY	☆ **Easy brain exercise** Teaching "Sit" first helps
PROPS	Your cat may have preferences. Often a soft carpet will increase the chances of success, but he may be more comfortable on a raised surface to start with.

4 The second your cat moves into a "Down" position, you should praise him and release the treat

Repeat a few times per training session until your cat can move quickly into the "Down" position when you move your hand downward

TIP
Remember that your cat will be unlikely to respond if he does not feel secure, so choose your training areas and timing carefully.

5 As he moves into position, start to say your "Down" or "Flat" verbal cue

With practice, your cat should start to be able to respond when you give the hand signal (the downward movement or point) but are no longer holding a treat in your hand

2 Crouch or sit beside your cat. Hold your treat between your fingers and bring it close to his nose to allow him to sniff and build up some interest.

Lower the treat slowly down to ground level, tempting your cat to try to follow it.

3 Hold your hand with the treat on the floor and wait patiently. Your cat is likely to try to get the food by sniffing, licking or pawing at your hand but should eventually move into a lying position to make it easier for himself.

6 Gradually work on reducing the signal down to smaller gestures so that you no longer have to actually touch the floor before your cat responds.

7 Always praise and reward him for responding to your directions. Keeping him engaged is vital!

Practice so your cat will respond even with outside distractions and in different locations.

A perfect "Down" position — don't forget to praise your cat for getting it right.

The hand movement is enough to lure this cat into a "Down."

45

STAND UP

While not the most exciting "game" per se, this lesson is very useful for times when you want your cat to change positions — perhaps when you are grooming or examining her and want to be able to feel all over her body. Knowing this response can also take some of the stress out of visits to the vet's office, since the position will already be associated with rewards and loving attention.

1 Your cat must be in either a sitting or a lying down position before you start

	INTERACTIVE GAME Cat and Owner
LOCATION	Anywhere
LEVEL OF DIFFICULTY	☆ Easy brain exercise
PROPS	Tasty treats or a toy

COME KITTY!

Although cats are renowned for doing their own thing, having a reasonably reliable signal to ask your cat to come to you is very handy. This will be useful in situations where you need to know where your cat is, or in emergencies if you should need to call your cat out of the house urgently, or if your cat is outside and you need to call him back indoors again. The key to having success with this lesson is to ensure that your cat is sufficiently rewarded to make him believe that responding to your call is worth his effort.

Ideally you need to be on the same level as your cat when you teach this. If it is not possible for you to get down to ground level, it is quite easy to teach it on a tabletop or a raised surface provided that it is safe for your cat to walk along it.

To repeat this lesson, you can wait for your cat to move some distance away from you, or toss a toy behind him so that he follows it. Then run through the lesson again after a few moments, making sure that you encourage and reward him for responding positively to you.

	INTERACTIVE GAME Cat and Owner
LOCATION	Begin in a quiet area of your home
LEVEL OF DIFFICULTY	☆ ☆ Moderate brain tester
PROPS	Treats

2 Approach and show her your treat or toy. Keep it just out of her reach so that she has to stretch to get to it. By doing so, she is likely to raise herself up. As she stands, praise her and offer the reward.

3 Once you can get your cat to stand up easily by luring her, you should introduce your verbal cue, "Stand." Say this each time just as your cat stands up, and she will pair up the action and the cue word.

Build this game up by gently touching her before you offer the reward, so that she realizes that standing results in a tasty treat.

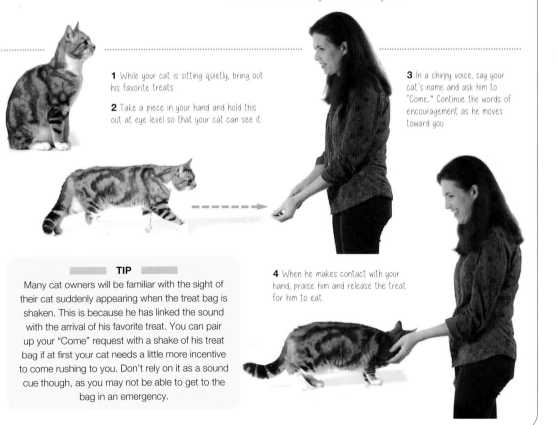

1 While your cat is sitting quietly, bring out his favorite treats.

2 Take a piece in your hand and hold this out at eye level so that your cat can see it.

3 In a chirpy voice, say your cat's name and ask him to "Come." Continue the words of encouragement as he moves toward you.

4 When he makes contact with your hand, praise him and release the treat for him to eat.

TIP
Many cat owners will be familiar with the sight of their cat suddenly appearing when the treat bag is shaken. This is because he has linked the sound with the arrival of his favorite treat. You can pair up your "Come" request with a shake of his treat bag if at first your cat needs a little more incentive to come rushing to you. Don't rely on it as a sound cue though, as you may not be able to get to the bag in an emergency.

SHAKE A PAW

Cats can be very aloof when they feel like it, but teaching your cat to shake a paw is fun, encourages interaction and can lead to other games too. Cats naturally use their feet to explore and to play so this game often does not take very long to teach, although each cat will differ with regard to the amount of contact they allow.

Lesson plan 1

1 Approach your cat when she is in the mood to engage with you and when she is interested in your treats.

2 Hold the treat in your hand, letting your cat see and smell it before closing your fingers around it. Hold this hand in front of your cat at head height, trying not to move your hand. Let her sniff and investigate to see if she can get to the treat. Typically a cat will then raise her foot to your hand to see if this helps her to get at the food. As soon as the paw makes contact with your hand, open it and let her have the food.

	INTERACTIVE GAME Cat and Owner
LOCATION	In a quiet area, preferably raised up for added security
LEVEL OF DIFFICULTY	☆ **Easy brain exercise**
PROPS	Tasty treats

Options There are two different ways to approach this game. Try not to jump between options, but first consider what stage your cat has reached. If she is already very confident about new tasks and readily uses her feet, then you can opt for lesson plan 1. For complete beginners and those cats that do not use their feet much, try lesson plan 2.

Lesson plan 2

1 Stand by your cat when she shows interest in engaging in some training.

You can play this game on the floor if you are prepared to crouch down, but it's generally more comfortable to work with your cat on a raised surface.

TIP

Cats do not usually touch one another's feet and so your cat may well feel sensitive about you touching and handling her paws. With careful and gradual handling she will begin to feel more comfortable with this action, but always remain aware that this is not a natural cat interaction. By teaching your cat to allow you to hold and check her feet and claws, you will be in a better position to examine and handle her when you need to in the future.

3 Repeat until the paw comes up each time you present food in your closed hand.

4 Begin to introduce the verbal cue "Shake" as the paw touches your hand.

5 When your cat is reliable at bringing her paw up to "Shake" yours, you can begin to practice without holding a treat. Instead, be ready to offer her a reward from your other hand when she gets it right.

And again, with the other paw!

Once you have mastered the "Shake" with one paw, try to encourage your cat to shake with the other as well. If your cat insists on only using one paw, encourage her to lift the other by using lesson plan 2 and focusing your practice on the unused paw.

2 Hold your treat in one hand ready to offer and with your other hand, lightly touch or tickle the top of the paw you wish her to raise, or "Shake." You will find that she shifts her foot in response to this contact. The second that foot moves, you should be ready to release the treat and praise her.

3 Repeat the touch and reward until you find that she is starting to lift her paw in anticipation.

4 Begin to increase the length of the paw touch while you offer the reward with your other hand.

Eventually you should be able to allow her paw to rest on your hand while you feed treats.

5 When she is confident at raising her paw up to your hand, you can introduce your "Shake" cue.

WAVE TO ME!

Cats can be such aloof animals that we are not surprised when they seem to take little notice as we come and go. So it may astonish your friends and family to see your cat waving!

Of course, this is not a game to try to force on a cat that is worried about people. However, for some, taking part in a game that they know and feel confident about can actually help them to feel surer of themselves. So this can be a helpful way of changing behavior for the better.

	INTERACTIVE GAME Cat and Owner
LOCATION	Anywhere. Surprise your guests by teaching your cat to wave at them!
LEVEL OF DIFFICULTY	☆ ☆ **Moderate brain tester** Teach "Kitty Sit" and "Shake A Paw" first
PROPS	Treats

1 Begin by teaching your cat to "Shake" as previously described.

Now reach out as if you are going to repeat the game, but this time keep your hand a little farther away from your cat than normal. This will entice him to reach out to touch you. Reward and praise him for making this effort.

REACH FOR THE SKY!

Most cats find sitting up on their haunches an easy skill, and so many of them should find this quite a simple game to learn. However, if your cat is elderly or is rather stiff when moving, it may not be the easiest skill to master.

Practice this game when your cat is feeling alert and confident.

	INTERACTIVE GAME Cat and Owner
LOCATION	In a quiet area, preferably raised up for added security
LEVEL OF DIFFICULTY	☆ **Easy brain exercise**
PROPS	Tasty treats

1 Begin with your cat in a standing or sitting position. Hold a treat between your fingers and let her see and sniff at it.

2 Slowly raise the treat so that your cat has to sit up higher in order to follow it. This will encourage her to rise up onto her haunches. When she does this, praise and feed her the treat.

1   2   3

2 Practice with your hand even farther from your cat so that his "reach" action becomes greater. Praise and reward him.

3 Add in your new verbal cue, "Wave," as your cat reaches out toward your outstretched hand. Offer a reward from your other hand to make sure that he continues to find this activity worthwhile.

Continue to practice in different areas of the house and then try while you are standing up so that your cat can respond to you in more natural circumstances. Eventually, when guests arrive at your house, you may be able to persuade your cat to wave Hello!

The hand movement lures the cat upward.

Up she comes onto her back legs.

3 With practice you can hold the treat higher so that your cat has to stretch up to touch your hand.

As you repeat this game, you should slowly increase the length of time your cat has to hold this position before you give the treat.

4 Introduce your verbal cue, "Reach." Begin to give the cue as you stretch out your hand toward your cat. If she has made the connection, she will respond by reaching up. Finally, practice with an empty hand, but always ensure that she is rewarded with praise or a treat for joining in.

ROLL OVER

Since your cat must be in a "Down" position to start this game, you must either wait until he lies down naturally, or teach the "Down" command first and then use it to encourage your cat into the correct starting position.

Some cats will naturally lie in a relaxed position with their weight shifted over to one side. This is great — you can use this position to decide which way you will teach the cat to roll over. However, if your cat is down with his legs tucked evenly underneath him, you will have to encourage him to move position slightly to make the game easier.

	INTERACTIVE GAME **Cat and Owner**
LOCATION	This must be taught in a location where your cat is secure. Working on a flat, stable surface is a great place to start.
LEVEL OF DIFFICULTY	☆ ☆ **Moderate brain tester**
PROPS	Tasty treats or a toy, a soft blanket or mat for him to roll on

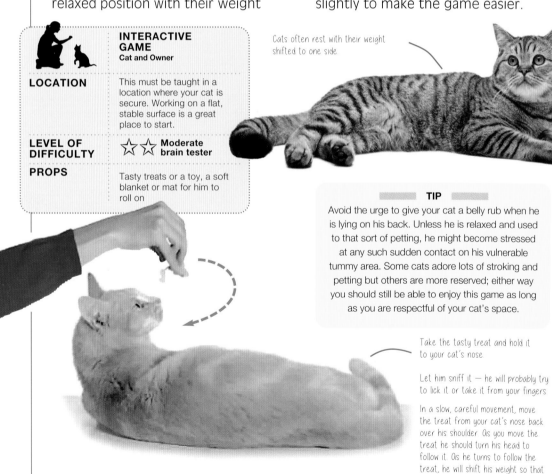

Cats often rest with their weight shifted to one side.

TIP

Avoid the urge to give your cat a belly rub when he is lying on his back. Unless he is relaxed and used to that sort of petting, he might become stressed at any such sudden contact on his vulnerable tummy area. Some cats adore lots of stroking and petting but others are more reserved; either way you should still be able to enjoy this game as long as you are respectful of your cat's space.

Take the tasty treat and hold it to your cat's nose.

Let him sniff it — he will probably try to lick it or take it from your fingers.

In a slow, careful movement, move the treat from your cat's nose back over his shoulder. As you move the treat he should turn his head to follow it. As he turns to follow the treat, he will shift his weight so that he is slightly over on one hip. Reward and praise him for doing this.

Take another treat and again hold it by your cat's nose.

1 Lure him around like before, only this time continue to move the treat so that your cat has to go over onto his shoulder, body flat on the floor, in order to get to it. Release the reward.

Once your cat can move into this position, you can progress to the next stage.

2 Practice this stage several times over your next training sessions so that your cat feels relaxed and secure on his side.

The next stage involves moving the treat all the way around and over to the other side, causing your cat to roll over as he tries to follow it. If he is successful at this, offer him his reward immediately.

3 Repeat until your cat can roll over quickly and reliably when you go to lure him around.

4 As he is rolling, start to introduce your cue phrase, "Roll Over."

With practice, over time your cat should become very proficient at this game.

5 Practice without a treat in your hand but be ready to offer him the reward from your other hand as soon as he completes the maneuver.

Eventually you can reduce the size of your hand gesture, so that you only need to give a small signal to see a beautiful response.

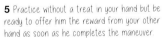

GAMES FOR MORE ACTIVE CATS

1 Hold a treat and allow your cat to focus on it before you begin

2 Hold the treat at around your cat's head height and move it in a circle so that she has to turn to follow it. When she has come the full 360 degrees in a circle, you should instantly release the treat for her to eat and praise her well

CAT SPIN!

Cats are agile and typically happy to engage in games that involve movement. In this game your cat can learn to spin around on cue. Whether your cat is a slow circler or a speedy twirler, this game can provide lots of fun for you both.

6 Over time you should start to reduce the emphasis of the hand signal, making the circle motion smaller and less obvious

Once your cat has learned this game, you might like to introduce some extra props, such as a colored cone, and teach her to spin around it

	INTERACTIVE GAME Cat and Owner
LOCATION	Choose a stable platform or safe area where your cat has space to turn around
LEVEL OF DIFFICULTY	☆ Easy brain exercise
PROPS	Tasty treats

3 Practice over several sessions until your cat is proficient at spinning to follow the treat lure.

4 Begin to give the cue word "Spin" as she moves around. Don't forget to praise and reward her each time.

5 Now give the same hand signal, but without holding a treat. Your cat should still get a reward at the end but should be less reliant on food being in your hand. She should respond entirely to the signal you give.

> **TIP**
>
> If your cat is reluctant to follow a food treat, you may want to use a feather or something she finds more interesting as a lure. Also, you can break down the spin into smaller movements that you reward in increments until she is turning the entire way around.

Mixing it up You may wish to introduce a second lesson, whereby you teach your cat to spin in the opposite direction to a different cue word. Avoid trying to teach these games at the same time, or you will both end up confused and without a clear response to the signals.

1 Use an excited tone of voice to entice your cat to approach you. Lure your cat up onto the chair by throwing a toy or treat onto it from your hand. Be ready to praise and reward when he lands on the chair.

2 Start to say "Up" (or something similar) just as your cat makes the jump up onto the surface. This will become your cue word and can be used in many different scenarios.

JUMP UP

I know, it doesn't exactly take high level training to get a cat to jump up on furniture! In fact, many owners spend a lot of time trying to stop their cats from getting onto certain things, and shooing them off beds and chairs where they are not wanted. However, it can be helpful to teach your cat to jump up onto a surface when you ask him to — perhaps in order to be groomed or checked by the vet, or as the starting point for another game that you wish to teach.

Health alert!

This game should not be a significant physical challenge, so if your cat is reluctant to jump up onto even low pieces of furniture, it would be sensible to ask your veterinarian to examine him. Many older cats have mobility problems as their joints become painful. They cover this up well, so often there are no signs other than a reluctance to get up on or down from raised surfaces.

	INTERACTIVE GAME Cat and Owner
LOCATION	Any room where your cat is comfortable
LEVEL OF DIFFICULTY	☆ **Easy brain exercise**
PROPS	A stable chair that your cat is allowed to jump on

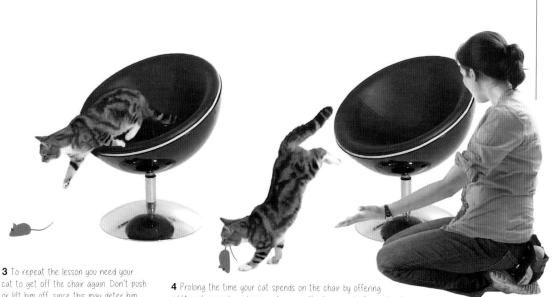

3 To repeat the lesson you need your cat to get off the chair again. Don't push or lift him off, since this may deter him from the game. Instead, say "Off you go" and toss the toy so that he jumps down to chase it.

4 Prolong the time your cat spends on the chair by offering additional rewards and praise. Increase the time gradually and try to give him a release cue such as "Off you go" when you are finished. Although most cats will stop playing the game when they feel like it anyway, it can help with the training to give clear signals indicating when you are done.

On a smaller scale

It is not wise to encourage a small kitten to jump up onto a high chair — if he falls, it could result in injury. Instead, you can enjoy an fun variation of the game using a prop like a cardboard box.

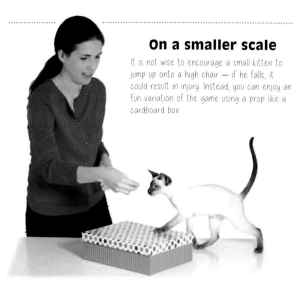

This kitten looks ready to Reach for the Sky!

1 Again, use a treat to lure the cat onto the lid of the box, but this time keep hold of it so that you have very precise control over how the cat is moving.

2 When he is in position, use the "Sit" command to get him nicely positioned and then release the treat as a reward.

JUMP OVER

Jumping is something that most cats relish having the opportunity to do. Young cats leap and jump at will but older cats may require more coaxing. Either way, most healthy cats can be taught to Jump Over without too much difficulty.

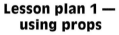

Lesson plan 1 — using props

1 Choose your prop. If it's a pole, lay this on the floor or flat on the surface you are working on. Allow your cat to explore the pole and familiarize herself with it. Lure your cat over the pole, praising and rewarding her as she steps over it.

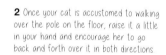

2 Once your cat is accustomed to walking over the pole on the floor, raise it a little in your hand and encourage her to go back and forth over it in both directions.

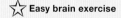

A small cheerleader's baton makes a very attractive hurdle.

INTERACTIVE GAME
Cat and Owner

LOCATION	In a safe area, but large spaces are not necessary — a tabletop will do nicely
LEVEL OF DIFFICULTY	☆ Easy brain exercise
PROPS	Treats and an object to jump over. This could be something like a broom handle or garden stake. If you do not have these on hand, you can use your legs and arms instead!

Lesson plan 2 — using legs and arms

1 Sit on the floor with your legs out in front of you.

2 Use a treat to lure your cat close and then over your leg. Praise her immediately and let her eat the treat.

3 After a few repetitions, if your cat is still keen to do more you can try to raise your leg a little. This might be by propping your foot on a cushion or by pressing your foot against a wall.

4 Add the cue "Over" as your cat makes the jump each time and remember to praise and reward her with her treat.

5 You can build up to a higher level by sitting with one leg propped on a chair for comfort.

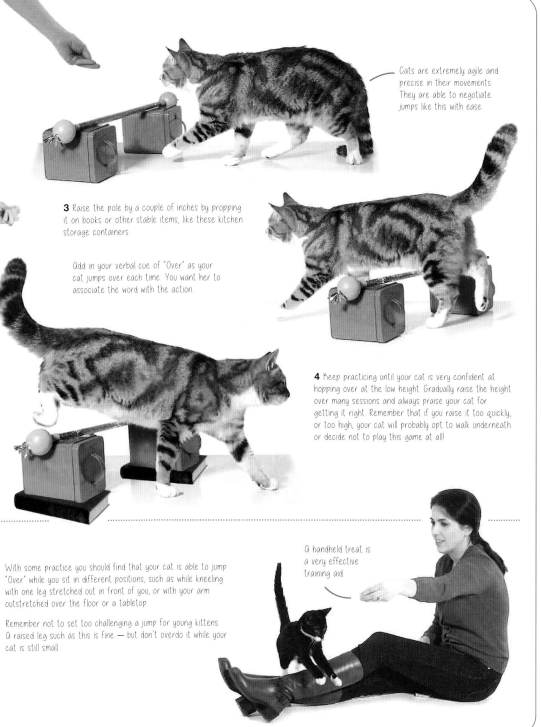

Cats are extremely agile and precise in their movements. They are able to negotiate jumps like this with ease.

3 Raise the pole by a couple of inches by propping it on books or other stable items, like these kitchen storage containers.

Add in your verbal cue of "Over" as your cat jumps over each time. You want her to associate the word with the action.

4 Keep practicing until your cat is very confident at hopping over at the low height. Gradually raise the height over many sessions and always praise your cat for getting it right. Remember that if you raise it too quickly, or too high, your cat will probably opt to walk underneath or decide not to play this game at all!

With some practice you should find that your cat is able to jump "Over" while you sit in different positions, such as while kneeling with one leg stretched out in front of you, or with your arm outstretched over the floor or a tabletop.

Remember not to set too challenging a jump for young kittens. A raised leg such as this is fine — but don't overdo it while your cat is still small.

A handheld treat is a very effective training aid.

THROUGH THE HOOP

Cats can be wary of new equipment and so it helps if you let your cat familiarize himself with the hoop before you start this game. Allow him to approach and sniff it well in advance so that there is no hesitation when you begin. Stand by the tabletop with the hoop held vertically and very steadily in front of you. Securely hold it with one hand — your other will be used to hold the treat or toy.

Walk through

1 Slowly use the toy or treat to lure your cat through the hoop. He may like to follow a moving item, so tossing a treat or toy can make him pounce through the hoop in chase. Praise him when he does so

Jump through

1 As your cat jumps through the hoop you can add in your cue word, "Hoop," and praise him

A cat is one of nature's supreme athletes. He can arch gracefully through the hoop

2 Start to very carefully raise the hoop a little from the surface level. Do so gradually and practice at each stage so that your cat is never put off hopping through. If you try to go too fast, he will opt to slip around or under the hoop instead of jumping through it. If he is unsure, go back to using the treat as an obvious lure rather than throwing it through and expecting him to leap after it

	INTERACTIVE GAME Cat and Owner
LOCATION	A safe area with a suitable, nonslippery surface
LEVEL OF DIFFICULTY	☆☆ **Moderate brain tester**
PROPS	A plastic or cardboard hoop and treats or a toy

2 Keep practicing over several sessions until your cat hops through the hoop when you ask him to.

PING-PONG PLAY

If you have a cat who loves a fast-paced chase game, this fun activity using lots of Ping-Pong balls is a great option.

1 Identify where you would like to play this game. Inside a box or in a bathtub works perfectly since the moving balls will ricochet and cannon around, creating more pandemonium and excitement.

2 Empty your pack of Ping-Pong balls into the play area. If your cat is sometimes anxious about new items, or has not played this before, it's probably best to start with just one or two balls.

3 Encourage your cat to enter the play area. She may dive in right away to chase the balls or, if more reluctant, have to be enticed in with a treat or a toy.

4 Once the excitement starts, you will be able to step back and let your cat enjoy the game all by herself.

Safe landings and he hasn't touched the sides!

TIP

If you are playing this game in the bathtub, make sure that all shampoos, soaps, razors and medications are put safely away. Keep an eye on your cat if you have lever-controlled taps; you will have to move fast if they are accidentally turned on.

3 With practice your cat's skill and confidence should grow with this game.

You will be able to try the game in different locations and in both directions.

	SOLO OR INTERACTIVE GAME Solo or Cat and Owner
LOCATION	Ideally in a location where the Ping-Pong balls won't all get lost under the furniture!
LEVEL OF DIFFICULTY	☆ Easy brain exercise
PROPS	Tasty treats, Ping-Pong balls

PURRFECT AGILITY

If you have taught your cat to Jump Up and to go Through The Hoop, then you should be able to make the transition to jumping on and over various items easily. By combining different obstacles on different levels, you will be able to create a type of mini agility course for your cat. He has a natural advantage for this type of sport, so as long as you make sure he is safe, and play within his physical and psychological limits, you can incorporate many things from around your home into this entertaining game. His inclination to join in will vary according to his mood and nature, but the more active, physical cats usually thoroughly enjoy this testing workout!

1 Start with low jumps over simple items, and build to more complex jumps and combinations of jumps as your cat progresses and grows more confident

LEFT Let your cat get accustomed to unfamiliar obstacles before you combine them in a course

2 Follow the guidelines given for the Jump Over and Through The Hoop games to accustom your cat to the idea of jumping over your chosen items

3 To pair up two or more jumps, you should follow straight on from the first and make sure that if your cat clears the second jump, he is rewarded very highly Remember that it has to be worth his while to put in the additional effort

4 Try to develop the game by linking various jumps with other physical challenges, such as climbs up a tall scratching post, dashes through a cat tunnel, and even weaving in and out of tight apertures like the spaces between the legs of a chair or a stool Over time you can create an energizing, stimulating and very exciting game Some cats get so good at this activity that their owners enter them for competitive agility events that are run against the clock Anyone who believes agility training games are only ever for dogs is very wrong!

	INTERACTIVE GAME Cat and Owner	
LOCATION	Cats do not need much run-up to perform a jump, so this can be played in most rooms — but avoid slippery surfaces	
LEVEL OF DIFFICULTY	☆☆☆	**Good brain workout**
PROPS	Many types of items can be included in this obstacle-course game	

Keep the treats and words of praise coming when you add a second element to a jump. Your cat needs to be fully motivated to keep going

Mission accomplished, so it's time for a treat

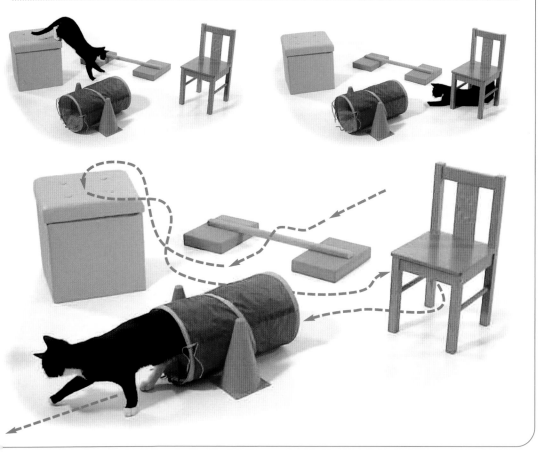

THE LEG WEAVE

Sometimes it can seem as if a cat's only goal in life is to wind around your legs and step between your feet at exactly the right moment to trip you up! This game takes this insidious habit and creates some structure and a cue signal around it. Getting a cat to perform a weave on cue is certainly impressive.

Having a treat in each hand will help you to keep the game running smoothly

1 A weave aims to teach your cat to move between and around your legs in a controlled fashion. Stand up and get your cat's attention by talking to her and showing her that you are holding a treat

2 Stand with your feet apart and bend to hold the treat near your cat's nose. Lure her through the gap from back to front and release the treat as she steps through

	INTERACTIVE GAME Cat and Owner
LOCATION	A place with enough floor space for your cat to step around and through your legs
LEVEL OF DIFFICULTY	☆ ☆ **Moderate brain tester**
PROPS	Treats

To get the full figure-eight maneuver, you will need to use both hands to keep the cat moving actively

4 If your cat is still engaged with the game, you can continue the figure-eight movement by luring with another treat in your other hand. Remember to release the treat as she moves through and around your legs

3 If she is still interested in the game, use your hand to lure her around the front of your leg again Release the treat as she moves around your leg

5 Practice over a few sessions until your movements are smoother and your cat becomes faster

As you practice, you can introduce your verbal cue, "Weave," so that eventually this will become the signal to get the game started

With sufficient practice your cat will start to respond when you simply make the hand gestures without even holding a treat. But remember that you must be ready to offer a reward as she completes the circuit, or she will lose interest and it will be game over

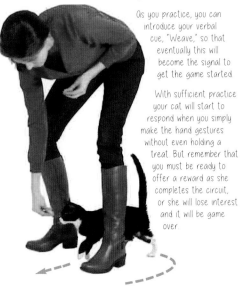

RELAXED WEAVE

Some owners find it more comfortable to teach a weave game while they are sitting down. This makes reaching down easier, as cats tend to be so small. You may also find that you have more opportunity to practice spontaneously when your cat approaches you when you are seated.

1 Use a treat to lure your cat around one chair leg Reward him for following your hand and offer the food as he moves through the figure-eight action

2 Break the movement into small elements and treat success with frequent rewards until your cat finds it easier to respond to your signals

Remember to give lots of praise and rewards so that your cat continues to enjoy this game and wants to play it with you

GAMES FOR CREATIVE OWNERS

Let's be honest, most cats find the mere presence of a box, or any similar sort of container, extremely tempting. If you don't already do so, I recommend that you provide opportunities for box-sitting around your home. Your cat might use them as a favorite resting spot, a hiding place, an ambush station or simply as a great place to play. While a basic, straightforward box can provide great amusement, with some alterations and additions box-

play can turn into a multidimensional entertainment system!

The act of making foraging toys for your cat is much more than just a "game." These playthings provide your cat with vital stimulation and help her to express natural exploratory, hunting and eating instincts. The beauty of these games is that you can either keep them very simple, or get a bit creative and introduce some mind-stretching variations.

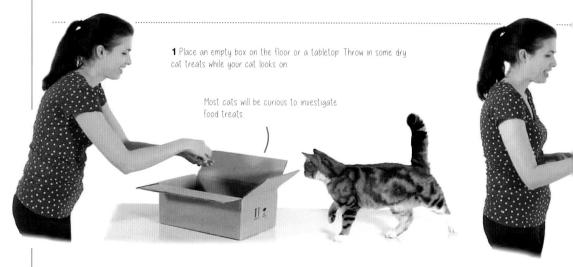

1 Place an empty box on the floor or a tabletop. Throw in some dry cat treats while your cat looks on

Most cats will be curious to investigate food treats

PURRFECTLY SIMPLE

Any type of cardboard box can be used in this game. When you've unpacked your parcel, the empty box and packing material can often be reused for your cat's benefit. Shoeboxes and even the boxes that hold wet food pouches can be put to brilliant new uses.

▬▬ **TIP** ▬▬
Used packing paper is great for this game, but avoid papers that are printed with inks that may be toxic to your cat, since any dyes or colorants that rub onto his coat will be licked and ingested.

Moving on To create a greater challenge for cats that love this game but need more stimulation, you should fill a box or shopping bag with cardboard tubes. The scattered treats and toys will disappear inside the tubes, fall out of the opposite ends and generally "escape" from your hunter for longer.

If you enjoy brain games with your cat, you will soon learn not to throw cardboard tubes away. They are great props for a variety of games. Here they turn a shopping bag into a miniature adventure playground.

The treats are somewhere in here!

2 Hopefully your cat will show interest and will approach. If he is already comfortable with boxes, he will probably jump right in.

3 Increase the challenge by closing part of the lid. Once your cat has hopped in and enjoyed his snack, he can relax in this hideaway. Your cat might prefer to enter the box via an entrance cut into the side.

	SOLO OR INTERACTIVE GAME Solo or Cat and Owner
LOCATION	An area where your cat feels relaxed
LEVEL OF DIFFICULTY	☆ Easy brain exercise
PROPS	A cardboard box, scrunched paper, cardboard tubes, toys, treats

4 Increase the challenge of the box game by adding scrunched-up paper to make finding the treats or toys a trickier task. Begin with one or two balls of paper and then add more as your cat becomes used to getting into the box with them. Of course, for some cats the paper will be a source of entertainment too.

CAT IN THE CASTLE

This game encourages your cat to take up residence in her own "castle" and then "defend" it from attack by a wiggly toy that you maneuver to make feint approaches to the castle windows.

	INTERACTIVE GAME **Cat and Owner**
LOCATION	An area where your cat feels relaxed
LEVEL OF DIFFICULTY	☆ **Easy brain exercise**
PROPS	A cardboard box and a wand toy, long ribbon or large feather. Scissors or a craft knife to cut holes in the box.

1 Take a box and cut an entrance hole and several smaller "windows" around each side and on top. These will be apertures that your cat will defend from attacks by your chosen toy.

Prepare with a selection of wand toys, ribbons or feathers close at hand.

It is best to use a large and sturdy box for the castle. Your cat will enjoy having room to twist and turn inside.

2 Position the box so you can access it from different sides. Encourage your cat to get inside the box using food treats or by attracting her interest with a wriggling toy. Alternatively, wait until your cat explores the box by herself.

3 Once your cat is inside the box, take one of the wand toys and draw the end across the box, passing in front of one of the windows. This should get your cat's attention.

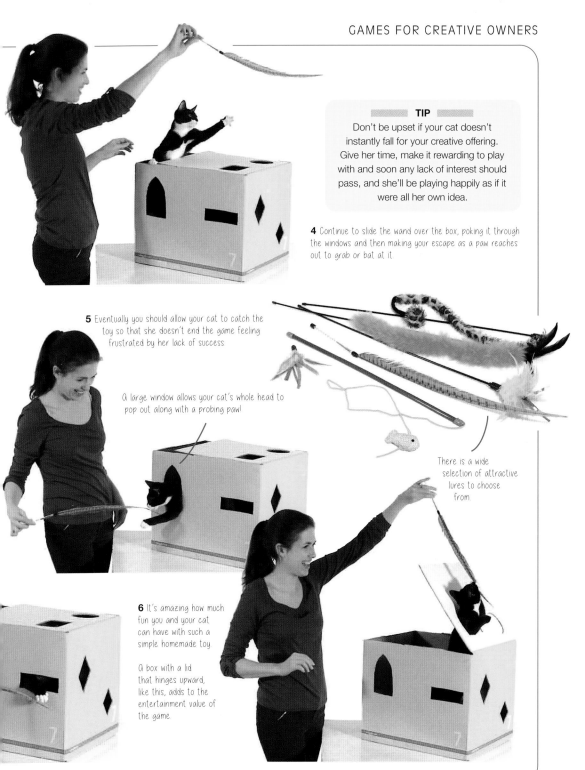

Don't be upset if your cat doesn't instantly fall for your creative offering. Give her time, make it rewarding to play with and soon any lack of interest should pass, and she'll be playing happily as if it were all her own idea.

4 Continue to slide the wand over the box, poking it through the windows and then making your escape as a paw reaches out to grab or bat at it.

5 Eventually you should allow your cat to catch the toy so that she doesn't end the game feeling frustrated by her lack of success.

A large window allows your cat's whole head to pop out along with a probing paw!

There is a wide selection of attractive lures to choose from.

6 It's amazing how much fun you and your cat can have with such a simple homemade toy.

A box with a lid that hinges upward, like this, adds to the entertainment value of the game.

LUCKY-DIP!

Roll up, roll up for the lucky-dip challenge! This is a simple game that is quick to prepare and easy to keep exciting. Everyone in the family can be

	INTERACTIVE GAME Cat and Owner
LOCATION	An area where your cat feels relaxed
LEVEL OF DIFFICULTY	☆ Easy brain exercise
PROPS	A cardboard box, treats and small toys. Scissors or knife to cut the holes in the box.

involved in maintaining the box's fun value for your cat by adding different treats and toys.

Take a small to medium-sized box and cut small holes around the sides. A large shoebox is ideal, although you can make do with most boxes or even plastic food containers. If you do use plastic, make sure the cut edges are not sharp.

NOVELTY BOX

Cats may take time to get used to new playthings, and their mood dictates what they do and don't find interesting at any particular time, so it is a good idea to have an arrangement whereby you rotate the provision of toys to keep playtime stimulating.

1 Take three or more small boxes and distribute your cat's small toys between them

Try to keep these selections varied in size and shape

	SOLO GAME Cat alone
LOCATION	Anywhere indoors or within a cat enclosure
LEVEL OF DIFFICULTY	☆ Easy brain exercise
PROPS	Three small containers and many small toy items

2 Your cat will want to explore, and has to reach inside the box to try to grab one of the goodies hiding in there

3 If you have a large cat that works out how to tip the box over to get the treats to all fall out at once, you may have to attach the box to a board or position it so that moving it around and tipping it over is difficult to do

1 Inside the box, hide a few small toys and delicious treats

TIP

Keep this game interesting by varying the prizes offered. Having lucky-dip stations scattered around the house is a great way to provide entertainment for your cat while you are away from home.

2 One set can be made available now, while the others are put away

3 Each week, collect up the toys from the first selection and put them away in their box. Swap this box with one from the cupboard

4 This means that the toys offered appear novel and interesting, rather than something your cat constantly sees and becomes bored with

TREAT TUBES

Need something to occupy your cat at the drop of a hat? This is an easy way to create a fun game that you can put together in just a minute. You can even get any children in the family to help with it. It's a good idea to make several tubes in advance and keep them aside until you need them.

1

2

	INTERACTIVE GAME **Cat and Owner**
LOCATION	Anywhere your cat likes to play
LEVEL OF DIFFICULTY	☆☆ **Moderate brain tester**
PROPS	A toilet roll inner tube, scrunched-up paper, treats or a catnip toy

1-3 Take a cardboard tube and crush one end so that it is almost completely closed

Then place a few treats into the open end before similarly crimping it shut Having both ends crimped closed will slow down the rate at which the treats are dispensed

Here's how to create quick and easy food dispensers that your cat can play with and rip apart before you recycle them and start again.

Making the game more challenging

As your cat gets to know the game and learns how to get the treats to spill out quite rapidly, you can start to increase the challenge. You are trying to make him work a bit harder and use his cognitive skills to figure out how to make the treats continue to fall out of the tubes.

1

1 Make the holes in the sides of the tube smaller (checking that they are still large enough for the treats to slip through when the tube moves around)

2 Put small balls of scrunched-up paper inside the tube to make it harder for the treats to fall out

2

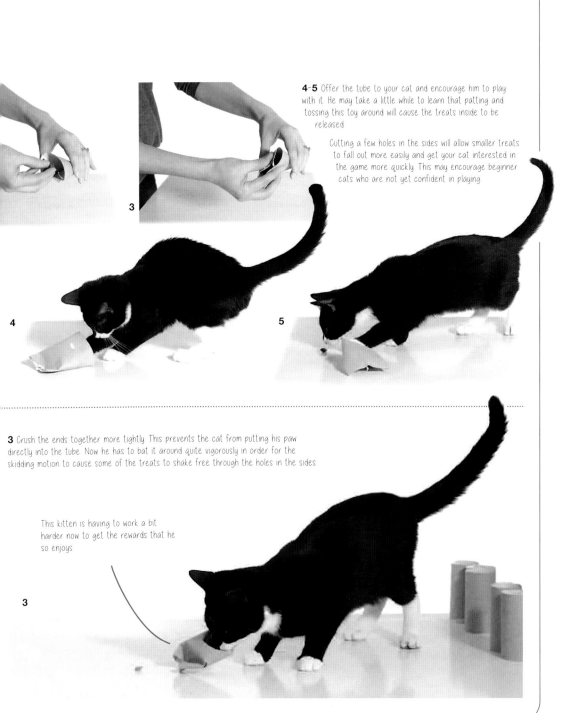

4-5 Offer the tube to your cat and encourage him to play with it. He may take a little while to learn that patting and tossing this toy around will cause the treats inside to be released

Cutting a few holes in the sides will allow smaller treats to fall out more easily and get your cat interested in the game more quickly. This may encourage beginner cats who are not yet confident in playing

3

4

5

3 Crush the ends together more tightly. This prevents the cat from putting his paw directly into the tube. Now he has to bat it around quite vigorously in order for the skidding motion to cause some of the treats to shake free through the holes in the sides

This kitten is having to work a bit harder now to get the rewards that he so enjoys

3

FORAGE FEEDER

This game is fun and also has health benefits. By offering some of your cat's food in a way that slows down her consumption while encouraging her to be more active, you can more easily manage weight programs and alleviate any problem behaviors relating to boredom and stress.

	INTERACTIVE GAME Cat and Owner
LOCATION	Anywhere safe and quiet where your cat can play and eat in peace
LEVEL OF DIFFICULTY	☆☆☆ **Good brain workout**
PROPS	Several toilet roll inner tubes, a cardboard lid or small box, animal-safe glue or adhesive tape, treats or small toys

Creating the foraging center

1 Cut your cardboard inner tubes to different sizes; some can be in half, some in thirds, some into a quarter or three-quarter length pieces. The aim is to have tubes of varying lengths to present your cat with different challenges.

2 Take a shoebox lid or small cardboard box and place the inner tubes inside to fill the space. If you use glue to attach them, make sure that the glued areas are not accessible by your cat, to avoid any risk of her chewing or licking and ingesting it. Tape is a great way to secure the tubes more safely, although you must still take care to position it so that your cat can't peel it off and chew on it.

A variation using paper cups

Adapting the game for cats with larger paws or less paw dexterity If your cat struggles to fit a paw inside a cardboard inner tube, then consider trying this alternative design.

1 Take a shoebox or other small box and some disposable paper or plastic or paper cups. Tape shut the lid or find the most secure side of the box and draw around your cups so that you have several circles where you would like your eventual foraging dips to be.

2 Using scissors, cut out those circles. (Cut them slightly smaller than the outlines so that your cups don't fall right through.)

3 You can then push in the cups from the outside so that they sit securely in the holes. Use tape to secure the cups in place. Once this has been done for all the cups, you can start the game.

4 Add treats to the cups and encourage your cat to explore the new foraging center.

Playing the game

3 The aim is to create a feeding center with towers of differing heights. When this is complete, and any glue has dried completely, you can drop some tempting cat treats or some of your cat's food into the tubes for your cat to find.

1 Encourage your cat to explore the new foraging center by waiting until she is hungry and then scattering the treats or food inside while she watches.

2 You may have to start with the easy, shorter tubes to begin with, but once your cat learns how to dip her paw in to scoop out the treats, she should be able to advance confidently to the trickier, taller tubes.

Even young kittens will enjoy dipping a paw into the surprise-laden cups to fish out a morsel to eat or an entertaining plaything.

A piece of meaty cat food tightly rolled into a ball makes an attractive treat for your foraging cat. This kitten has been able to grasp the food with just one paw by dextrous use of his claws. With practice, even quite small, hard treats, like biscuits or kibble, can be fished out successfully.

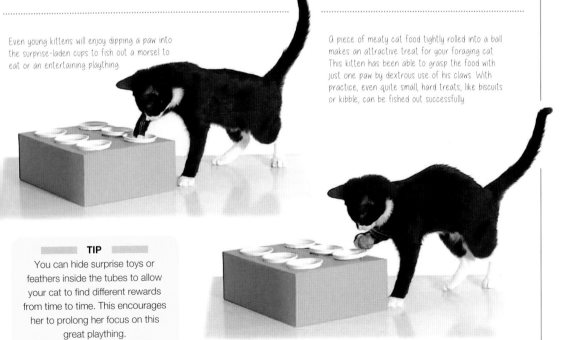

TIP
You can hide surprise toys or feathers inside the tubes to allow your cat to find different rewards from time to time. This encourages her to prolong her focus on this great plaything.

GAMES FOR THE YARD OR A CAT

The rules about allowing your cats outdoors will depend on where you live and your own personal choice. The benefit of allowing cats more freedom is that they can express their natural feline instincts outdoors and will therefore often be more satisfied individuals. Of course, those same feline instincts may be the exact reason why you decide to prevent your cat from free-roaming — will he come home safe and sound? If you prefer to keep your cat indoors, your challenge is to find ways to allow him to perform the activities he naturally loves, but in a safe environment and a neighborhood-friendly manner. Remember that if your cat does roam loose but finds lots of entertainment in his own backyard, he may be less inclined to stray far and will have less opportunity to get into trouble.

Whether your cat has access to your yard or is confined within a cat enclosure, you can still enrich this environment and allow him to play very easily. When outdoors, a cat wants to feel safe and secure. For this reason, any recreational area that you create for your cat must allow him to feel secure and relaxed while he explores and plays in it.

CONCEAL THAT CAT!

Cats just love finding secret hideaways where they can tuck themselves away. This might be because they want to watch the world go by unnoticed, to hide from something they are not sure about or often simply for a nap.

	SOLO GAME Cat alone
LOCATION	In your cat enclosure or around your yard
LEVEL OF DIFFICULTY	☆ Easy brain exercise
PROPS	Plant pots, troughs, boxes, paper bags

The key to creating nice hiding places is to think about your cat's area carefully, and from her perspective. If you find it difficult to imagine what

ENCLOSURE

she's thinking, it may help to actually get down on the floor to look around from her point of view. Cats consider their world from both a horizontal and a vertical viewpoint. Since it is natural for them to climb and leap, this makes perfect

sense. Humans, however, tend to assess spaces by how much floor space they offer. We do not often climb or seek out elevated resting areas, and by missing this dimension we ignore areas that are potentially important to our cats.

How many hideaways should you provide? Give your cat plenty of choice — different options to choose from will keep her much happier.

Going up a level

Your cat will appreciate some areas to tuck herself away at ground level, but don't forget to include some raised options — for instance by securing a

box on a raised platform, on a shelf fixed to a fence or wall, or on a roof. How you create a space for your cat will depend on the area you have available.

Into the jungle

Another way to create wonderful hiding and play areas is to place foliage in strategic places around your yard, or within your cat's enclosure. These can be leafy plants grown in pots or planted directly into the ground. These create screens for her to hide behind.

CAUTION!

While there are many completely safe plants, some are toxic to cats, so please research which plants you intend to put in your cat's play area before you introduce any.

FIND THE FOOD

In the wild, your cat would naturally use search and hunt behavior in order to find his food. In the domestic home, this activity usually becomes irrelevant, as we place bowls of food out in a specific place, at certain times of day. This game will help your cat to engage in more natural instinctive behavior before consuming some of his favorite foods.

1 Measure out the amount of treats or dry food that you want to use in this game. Take the food into the enclosure before your cat is let into this area

2 Position small amounts of treats in various places around the area, so your cat will discover them as he explores the enclosure. Initially you may want to make this easy so that he has early success

 **SOLO GAME** Cat alone	
LOCATION	In your cat enclosure, around your yard (or even indoors)
LEVEL OF DIFFICULTY	☆ **Easy brain exercise**
PROPS	Some of your cat's favorite treats

3 As he gets better at the game, you can hide the food in places that are more difficult to access

I'M FOREVER BLOWING BUBBLES!

This is one of the simplest games in this book, but it can provide lots of fun for cat and owner alike. Children love playing this game too, although care must be taken to ensure that they do not rush around trying to chase and grab bubbles and in the process trip over your cat.

In an open area with your cat nearby, blow some bubbles from the bubble blower, and then watch her reaction!

You might want to consider purchasing a child's battery-powered bubble maker for faster production; this is especially useful if your cat adores this game!

	INTERACTIVE GAME Cat and Owner
LOCATION	In your cat enclosure or yard
LEVEL OF DIFFICULTY	☆ **Easy brain exercise**
PROPS	Cat-safe bubble solution, bubble blower

Increase the challenge

Start to place some of the food underneath paper cups and plates. He should be interested if he knows that food is involved.

Use a light plastic bowl that your cat will be able to move easily

First of all you will need to show your cat that there are goodies waiting underneath, but once he has gained some experience of this activity, your cat should be able to explore and seek out the food for himself

In this case, curiosity feeds the cat!

CLIMBING CAT

Your cat's natural instinct means that he wants to climb when he has the opportunity. He knows how to climb but he may require some practice to become really proficient. With encouragement and when he discovers the pleasures of relaxing areas up high, or prizes to discover, your cat will be happily climbing within a short time.

You may be lucky enough to have a perfectly positioned tree in your backyard, but for most people it will probably be easier to create a climbing area with a large log or branch that can be positioned somewhere convenient, safe and suitable for your cat.

The log can be used in different ways depending on your cat.

Start with the log positioned flat on the ground

1 Position it horizontally and allow your cat to explore. He may use it to scratch, which is a great way to stretch his muscles and to perform a natural feline behavior

2 Secure the log with a slight slope so that your cat can practice scaling it. Encourage him to climb and jump up by luring him up with a toy or a treat. Getting him to chase a wand toy is a great way to engage a cat and get him jumping and leaping around

To create even more interesting climbing options you can create a "ladder" setup; recycling sections of old wooden ladders is a great way to put them to an exciting new use. If you are bit of a DIY expert, you may be able to make one yourself just by using spare lumber. Wrapping the steps or rungs with old carpet is a simple way to make the climbing frame attractive to a less confident climber. It is not so slippery, and easier for less agile cats to climb. Old carpet scraps are perfect for this and you can replace them yearly as they get worn out.

RIGHT Cats are astonishingly agile climbers and will readily scale quite precipitous heights. DIY enthusiasts can even create a custom-made stepladder from offcuts of wood

	SOLO OR INTERACTIVE GAME Solo or Cat and Owner	
LOCATION	In your cat enclosure or backyard	
LEVEL OF DIFFICULTY	☆ Easy brain exercise	
PROPS	A tree or a large log or branch	

You do not need to spend a fortune on a ready-made climbing center for your cat. A sturdy branch rigged up securely in the backyard or cat enclosure will serve just as well.

...ke sure that it is nice and ...ady when the cat first ...plores it.

A branch also doubles as a scratching post.

A feather lure is a great way to get a cat excited and eager to leap onto the log.

3 You may wish to increase the slope of the log or eventually to secure it in an upright position. The choice is yours, although you should observe your cat's natural habits and try to create a climbing option that suits his physical ability and preferences. As cats grow older, they lose some suppleness and mobility, so be prepared to make allowances.

NOTE

It is of course possible to purchase some wonderful ready-made cat climbing centers, but these are often better for indoor use. Do try to create climbing areas indoors as well as outside, so that your cat can freely express this part of his natural personality.

PIÑATA FUN

Piñatas are a common element of celebrations and fun. They are usually decorated containers made of paper or pottery that are filled with treats and sweets. When you strike them, the treats spill out. You can create a simple version to entertain your cat. Hanging toys are not recommended for cats that are unsupervised, but there are ways to create safe versions.

	SOLO OR INTERACTIVE GAME Solo or Cat and Owner
LOCATION	In your cat enclosure or backyard
LEVEL OF DIFFICULTY	☆ ☆ **Moderate brain tester**
PROPS	You will need a raised place to secure the toy, a paper bag or even a takeout cup and lid. A selection of treats, small toys and some dried catnip if your cat enjoys it.

Paper bag

Paper bags can provide many play opportunities for most home situations. They can easily provide fun while a cat is within her enclosure too.

1

4 Alternatively, you can make a hole through the upper part of the bag and loop through a plastic shower-curtain hook or a climbing carabiner, which allows you to attach the treat piñata to a secure point in the enclosure or yard. You could also use a clamp to fix the bag to a convenient spot.

3

1 Take a paper bag and remove any handles, as since these could potentially harm your cat if she were to get her head or a leg stuck through the loop. Cut some very small holes around the sides and bottom to allow your cat to sniff the goodies inside.

2 Place treats and toys inside, and roll down the top so that they are secure inside and won't spill out too easily.

3 For a very simple game, the bag can then be placed on the floor for your cat to play with and even climb into.

2

You can adapt this game so that your cat can play it in a covered area like an enclosed porch or a greenhouse by using items of furniture, like this bar stool, as anchor points for the piñata

CAUTION!

It is essential to avoid playing any type of game that could result in injury to your cat. While this game would be easy to create using elastic or strings to hold the treat bag or cup, please **do not leave your cat unsupervised** with these items or any other small parts that could be chewed off. It is not recommended to hang up any toy for a cat that will be playing with it by herself without supervision.

The kitten learns how to get treats to drop out of the bag

As your cat becomes more confident at this game and knows what to expect, you could skip the step of making holes in the bag before presenting it to her, or start to hang it in more challenging places. Attaching the piñata to branches or ledges within her run makes this a challenging game to play

OVER THE BRIDGE

Cats generally have great balance, so this game that involves walking across a wooden bridge should not pose too many problems for your cat. As his skill and confidence increase, you can build this element into a bigger overall agility display. For further ideas about combining various obstacles in an agility course, see pages 62–63.

1 Place the plank or "bridge" item on a stable surface where it will not wobble.

2 Encourage your cat to come to one end and, using a treat to lure him, guide him to step onto the plank. The aim is for your cat to walk the length of the plank without stepping off. You may need to build up this skill in stages depending on the cat's confidence.

3 Start to move ahead of your cat so that the lure is farther from him and he is generally following the movement of your hand.

4 Eventually your cat should only get the reward when he successfully gets to the other end of the bridge.

5 Start to practice without any food in your hand, but still be prepared to offer the reward for especially good responses.

6 Once your cat is confident at responding to this game you can start to add in your cue, "Bridge."

	SOLO OR INTERACTIVE GAME Solo or Cat and Owner
LOCATION	You can start this inside your home, but it could easily be adapted to suit your cat's enclosure or your backyard
LEVEL OF DIFFICULTY	☆ ☆ **Moderate brain tester**
PROPS	A plank of wood or similar sturdy wooden board, treat rewards, possibly a toy to use as a lure

Moving on

Carefully raise the bridge either by propping it securely on heavy books or yoga blocks, or by placing it between two low stools or chairs.

The options are numerous and will depend on the location in which you are playing, the available props and the abilities of your cat.

1 A couple of yoga blocks provide a good solid base when you start to raise the bridge off the work surface. As the cat grows in confidence, you may add more blocks to increase the height of the bridge.

2 A food treat is an ideal lure to encourage a cat to walk over the bridge toward you

Carnival cat

Combining several fun activities can create opportunity for exercise and mental stimulation. It will undoubtedly provide an impressive display for any family and friends watching the show. You can adapt this game to suit your cat's preferences, ability and level of training.

Here's one idea: link up different games in a sequence — for instance, Jump Up, Over The Bridge, Through The Hoop, and then Wave To Me! And end with your cat sitting on the "Winner's" podium as a grand finale to the entertainment!

ABOVE Once a cat is confidently crossing a bridge, you can introduce extra elements into the game — like a hoop

85

GAMES FOR EXTROVERTED CATS

You may have already explored the fun world of target training with another pet, usually a dog, but perhaps you have not considered applying the method to your cat. This chapter shows you how to target train a cat. As with most of the games in this book, teaching this skill to a cat does pose additional challenges, but with patience and practice the results can be extremely satisfying.

CLICKER

Target training is enhanced by the use of a clicker (see Chapter 3). This tells your cat at the exact moment he touches the target that he has performed a desirable behavior. If you don't want to use an actual clicker, you can replace the signal with a well-timed word of praise such as "Yes!" or "Good!" or you can even use a tongue "cluck" as a signal for your cat. These can be introduced in the manner explained for using the clicker described in Chapter 3.

PAW TARGET

This game teaches your cat the basics of touching a target with her paw when requested to do so. The clicker is used to reinforce your response to the correct action, which will bring a reward.

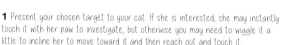

Targets can take all kinds of forms. This brightly colored disk is also used for target training dogs

1 Present your chosen target to your cat. If she is interested, she may instantly touch it with her paw to investigate, but otherwise you may need to wiggle it a little to incline her to move toward it and then reach out and touch it.

2 Immediately sound your clicker or say "Good!" and reward your cat.

It helps to wiggle the target to attract your cat's attention

	INTERACTIVE GAME Cat and Owner
LOCATION	Indoors, where your cat is relaxed
LEVEL OF DIFFICULTY	☆ 1-3 stars ☆ ☆ ☆ This varies depending on how you apply the target activity
PROPS	Targets such as nonslip coasters, Post-it notes, colored adhesive tape, laminated card patches

A nose touch signifies interest, but only click and reward a paw touch

4 Start to place the target down a few inches in front of your cat. If she has learned that touching the target brings a reward, she should move forward to touch it. When she does, click and reward her as usual.

5 Start to give a cue to encourage your cat to go to the target. This could be the word "Touch" but some cats will also work to a clear hand signal. As your cat touches the mark, say your cue word and reward.

6 Over several practice sessions you can move the target farther from your cat so that she has to cover a greater distance in order to touch it.

7 Continue to practice, saying the cue word while she is on her way to the target mark. Eventually she will link the cue with the action of going to touch this mark.

8 With sufficient practice, your cat should be able to move toward the target and touch it in different locations around your house. Of course, this will depend on the level of distractions around her, and the amount of practice you have been able to put in.

With practice and regular rewards, the cat will learn that a paw touch is the desired reaction

3 Repeat the exercise a few times to encourage your cat to touch it with her paw. Each time she should earn a reward. Over a few short training sessions, your cat should become increasingly confident in touching this target with her paw.

Direction matters

You should think about how you want to use the target. Will you generally prefer your cat to be moving away from you, or toward you to touch it? Then shape your practice to suit this action.

INTO YOUR CARRIER

While the paw targeting skill can be used to enjoy many games with your cat, you can also put it to practical use to help your cat step more willingly in and out of his cat carrier. Traveling in a carrier can be stressful for cats, so having a way to lessen their anxiety can be extremely helpful.

> ### TIP
>
> Ideally you should have a different target for each different action. For example, you may wish to have a target that your cat places his paw on, another that he lies on and another he touches with his nose. You should decide how you want to use your targets and keep a note of what you are using them for to avoid confusing your cat.

1 If possible, take apart your carrier so that only the base part remains. Practice the paw target touch near the carrier to help your cat become accustomed to it. If he is already very worried by the cat carrier, then you need to leave it around for a few days so that he can get used to its presence before you try to train him around it

5 Once your cat will enter the carrier, resist the urge to close the door right away. Your aim should be to help your cat learn that the carrier is a nice place to spend time

Once you are sure that he likes the space, you can begin to close the door briefly while he eats the treats, and then increase the time gradually so that he never feels trapped and panicked

2 Move the target closer to the box and then gradually try placing it just inside the base of the carrier so that your cat has to step in to touch it Work within your cat's comfort zone and do not be tempted to push him faster than he is happy to go

3 Continue to practice getting your cat to step into the base of the carrier until he can go fully into it while remaining happy and calm

4 The next step involves replacing the top part of the carrier Allow your cat to familiarize himself with it, and then ask him to touch the target at the entrance, then move the target to the back of the box to attract him inside He can earn a jackpot prize for succeeding here

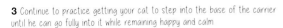

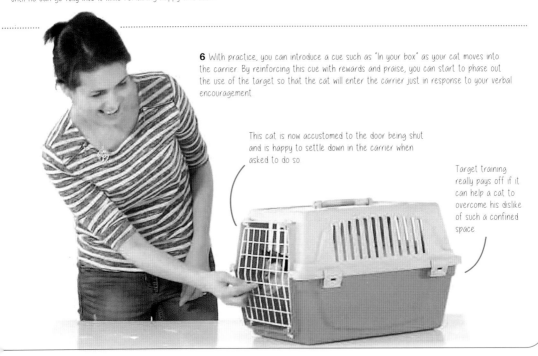

6 With practice, you can introduce a cue such as "In your box" as your cat moves into the carrier By reinforcing this cue with rewards and praise, you can start to phase out the use of the target so that the cat will enter the carrier just in response to your verbal encouragement

This cat is now accustomed to the door being shut and is happy to settle down in the carrier when asked to do so

Target training really pays off if it can help a cat to overcome his dislike of such a confined space

RING FOR ROOM SERVICE

Many amusing cat stories hinge on the idea that cats are the "masters" and we owners mere household staff engaged in satisfying their every desire. This game features an activity that plays on this notion. One way of using your "paw target" lesson is to teach your cat to tap on a bell. While most cats are very capable of letting us know when they want something from us, by teaching your cat to ring the bell you can make the signal crystal clear and also create a game that will amaze your guests!

Initially you teach the target touch on its own and then introduce the bell

1 Ideally you should teach your cat to use her paw to touch the target before you introduce the bell. Focus on the kind of movement that your cat is using for the touch. If you have encouraged a sideways swipe rather than a downward tap, then she might need to spend some time being encouraged to press down on the target marker to earn the reward. Once you have taught the appropriate paw action in relation to your chosen target, the target can be attached to the ringer of the bell (*right*)

2 Practice getting her to touch the target close to the bell. At first it is sensible to ensure that the bell does not ring loudly and frighten your cat away from the game — if possible, muffle the sound. If this is not an option, then let your cat become accustomed to the ringing sound from a distance before gradually moving it closer. If you pair up the sound with the arrival of a treat, your cat will learn to associate the ring with a pleasurable outcome

3 When your cat touches the target while it rests on the bell, click and treat. At first she does not need to press hard enough to ring it. Repeat so that she is comfortable with this part of the lesson

	INTERACTIVE GAME Cat and Owner
LOCATION	In a place with few distractions, ideally near where you eventually want your cat to perform this trick
LEVEL OF DIFFICULTY	☆☆☆ **Good brain workout**
PROPS	Target marker, clicker, a tabletop bell and treats

A good firm press will make the bell ring

4 You now want to encourage her to put more effort into the touching action. By delaying the praise and reward it is likely that your cat will try again, usually with a bit more pressure due to a little buildup of frustration. This action can then be rewarded well. Over time and with practice your cat should only earn the reward for a touch that has sufficient force behind it.

Right on cue! Now for a well-earned reward.

5 As your cat becomes competent at hitting the bell, you can introduce your cue phrase, "Ring it," just as she strikes the bell. Keep practicing until she can ring the bell on cue.

7 If you initially muffled the sound of the bell, you can begin to remove the muffling now that your cat feels confident in touching it. When the bell first actually rings, you should be ready to offer tasty rewards immediately. She will soon connect the sound and expect something nice to occur whenever she hears the bell ring.

6 You eventually want to withdraw the target marker (above) so that your cat is ringing the actual bell. How you do this will depend on what you have used as a marker. A card marker can be cut down into ever smaller pieces while you practice, until you are working with only the bell itself. If you are working with a target stick, then you can position the target just out of reach so that your cat has to stretch over the bell to get to it. Be ready to "click" your cat when she touches the bell instead of the target stick. After a while she should realize that she is being rewarded for touching the bell instead of the marker.

TIP

You might want to encourage your cat to ring the bell before you offer her food, or before you open the door. However, you should remove the bell when you are not around so that your cat does not attempt to ring it while you are absent. If you don't take this precaution, you could risk her becoming frustrated at the lack of response and then choosing to ignore the game in future. Another reason for removing the bell when not actively playing is that cats have very different sleep-wake patterns from humans and it is quite possible that you will start to hear an unwelcome "ding-ding" in the night when your cat fancies a snack!

IT'S UNDER YOUR NOSE

Teaching your cat to move to touch your hand or a specific target can be both mentally stimulating and useful in a practical way. By teaching your cat to anticipate a pleasurable experience when you ask him to touch your hand or a target with his nose or head, you can get him to move willingly from one location to another with a minimum of fuss.

1 Present your chosen target in front of your cat. It should be a few inches away so that it is not too close to worry your cat, but not so far that he cannot easily reach it with his nose. If your cat is interested in playing the game, he will probably lean over to sniff the target.

2 Offer the target again and once more click and treat when your cat touches it with his nose or head. You might have to move it slightly to get his interest, but this is not a grab-it game so do not wiggle the target like you would a toy.

At this precise moment you should click and treat, or use your praise word, 'Good,' and offer the treat.

Click and treat when he head-bumps the target

INTERACTIVE GAME
Cat and Owner

LOCATION	Choose a location where your cat is comfortable. Often a raised surface is the best place to begin.
LEVEL OF DIFFICULTY	☆ 1-3 stars ☆☆☆ This varies depending on how you apply the target activity
PROPS	Your hand or a target, plus a clicker and treats

3 Repeat the offer of the target and the reward a few more times. If your cat typically gets bored quickly, then keep this session very short and return to it after a break.

Different applications

Once your cat is confident in playing this game, you can start to apply it to different settings. Remember to take things slowly when you change location or involve new props. You can use this nose-touch action to encourage your cat to move around an obstacle course, allowing him to target your hand or the stick at key stages. On a more practical level, you can use the nose touch to encourage your cat to step onto a scale. A significant number of pet cats are overweight and so it is helpful to be aware of your cat's changing weight over his lifetime. While you can pick him up and make him stand on a scale, he will probably want to get off as soon as he can, and if you hold him to make him stay, you will affect the reading. Instead, teach your cat to step onto the scale himself in order to make contact with your target. This is a calmer and less stressful way of approaching the task.

Another amusing variation is to play Who's Your Favorite? — it's a fun way to let all your family see who your cat's favorite person is. It's a simple trick if you use the chosen cue word or signal. Innocently ask your cat "Who's your favorite?" while giving the hand gesture that means your cat should come and bump his head against you. A bit sneaky, but if you have put in all the time training, then you've probably earned the accolade!

4 Present the target in a slightly different position. This may be higher, lower or to a different side from the original position. Reward as usual as soon as your cat makes contact.

You can add variation to the nose touch by moving the target around.

5 As your cat starts to become faster at touching the target, you can begin to place it a little farther away from him so that he has to move in order to make contact.

6 Ideally you want to encourage a firm contact, so once your cat is confident at touching it, you should start to hold back the click or the "Good" until he bumps it a bit harder. Be careful though, because if you expect too much too soon and withhold rewards for too long, your cat is likely to lose interest.

7 Introduce a verbal cue for this game. Avoid using the word "Touch" if you are using this for another action, such as a paw touch. Instead use a novel cue word, like "Bump it!," spoken with suitable enthusiasm!

8 Over time you should be able to present your target some distance away from your cat and he should be happy to go over and "Bump it!"

TAKING IT LYING DOWN

This game teaches your cat to lie down on a particular target. This is not usually difficult to achieve, especially if the chosen target is something your cat likes to lie on. You can then use the target to teach your cat to go and lie down on a particular spot. This game works well with active cats. More sedentary cats can also learn it, but they are unlikely to find themselves particularly motivated by having to lie down, get up and lie down again so don't expect miracles!

Use a target that isn't going to slip on the work surface

1 Position the target mat and lure your cat into a "Down" on it. Reward her for doing so

There are real, practical benefits in teaching your cat to lie on a target wherever it may be positioned

	INTERACTIVE GAME Cat and Owner
LOCATION	Anywhere familiar to your cat; preferably on a raised surface to begin with
LEVEL OF DIFFICULTY	☆ 1-3 stars ☆ ☆ ☆ This varies depending on the cat's ability and your application. It helps if you have already taught your cat the "Down" command.
PROPS	A nonslip mat is excellent for this game. Remember that you want to keep this item for other "Down" target training.

4 When she is reliably lying down on the target, start to introduce your cue word or phrase. "Get on it" works well and is different from the other commands. With practice, you can move the target to different places and encourage your cat to go and lie on it

When she does lie down, allow your cat a few seconds of contentment before you ask her to do it all over again

Useful applications

This skill can help when it comes to grooming or if it's time for a medical examination. You can also try placing the target marker in the cat carrier — this should encourage your cat to enjoy using this space and not feel stressed when she is asked to go inside.

2 Distract your cat from the target mat and then after a short break, encourage her back and repeat the 'Down' action and reward again

3 Each time that your cat lies on the target, she should be praised and rewarded

Gradually fade out the target by making it smaller

Moving on You can fade out the target over time by using a smaller and smaller marker for your cat to find. Some cats work really well this way, and in the end the action itself, performed in the particular place where it has been rewarded, becomes the thing that your cat learns to repeat. Alternatively, you can start to place the reward beyond the point where you want your cat to go and make sure that you click and reward before she makes contact. In this way, the act of going to a place and performing the desired action is being rewarded and eventually the target itself can be removed.

5 If she is unsure at first, begin by rewarding her for approaching the mat and touching it in some way. Once she has learned that it holds some interest, move on to encouraging her to lie down before the reward is offered

ACKNOWLEDGMENTS

A big thank you to everyone who supported me in the writing of this book. I greatly appreciate the patience of my husband and son who tolerated my long hours at the computer, and who made the non-working hours so much fun. Thanks to my very good friend Ruth who read through all the first drafts of my books and helpfully gave constructive suggestions. I am also very grateful to the production team for the opportunity and time to complete this book.

A very important mention must go to Ace Cat Rescue in Surrey, U.K., for providing all the beautiful cats that took part. Feline photoshoots are not easy to orchestrate smoothly and the cats were absolutely wonderful. I sincerely hope that trainer and rescue owner Sue Ottmann continues to be able to help unwanted cats find their way into new homes.

PICTURE CREDITS

Unless otherwise credited here, all the photographs in the book were taken for, and are the copyright of, Interpet Publishing.

Shutterstock.com
Evgeniia Abisheva: 21 bottom
absolutimages: 26 top right, 34 bottom (cat)
afitz: 80 left
Ermolaev Alexander: 12 bottom, 13 top, 21 top, 29 bottom, 36 (both pictures), 38 (all pictures), 93 top (cat)
Aliwak: 9 top (mouse)
Khomulo Anna: 25 top (cat)
ANP: 11 bottom
Bloomua: 30 bottom (phone)
Elena Butinova: 20 bottom
Tony Campbell: 10 top, 11 top, 18 top right, 37 bottom
Mark Caunt: 76
Linn Currie: 22 bottom
cynoclub: 31
eZeePics: 30 top
5 second Studio: 28 bottom
greenphile: 93 top (scale)
Eric Isselée: 10 bottom left, 22 top (cat), 27 top (cat), 77 top (cat), 95 center (cat)
vita khorzhevska: 32 top
Rita Kochmarjova: 14 left
Denys Kurbatov: 77 bottom (bubbles)
Andrey_Kuzmin: 17 center (kittens)
Oksana Kuzmina: 12 top, 79 bottom (kittens)

Lenkadan: 81 bottom right
Lepas: 8
Natalie Lukhanina: 18 top left
Madlen: 77 top (herbs)
mashimara: 77 bottom right
Malyshev Maksim: 94 center (cat)
mdmmikle: 28 top
My Good Images: 9 top (cat)
Okssi: 79 top (cats)
Sari ONeal: 77 center left
Martina Osmy: 19 top
photomak: 13
Vic and Julie Pigula: 16 top (kitten)
Anurak Pongpatimet: 16 bottom left
Anucha Pongpatimeth: 24 bottom (cat)
pryzmat: 33 (hands)
Julia Remezova: 9 bottom left
Fesus Robert: 23
rysp_z: 9 center right
Atiketta Sangasaeng: 77 top (shrub)
schankz: 26 bottom left
Voronina Svetlana: 77 top (grass)
Diana Tallun: 37 top
Tanee: 52 top
Nikolay Titov: 43 bottom (kitten)
Ivonne Wierink: 17 center (toy)
Sonsedska Yullia: 33 (cat), 81 bottom left
yykkaa: 15 top